Grindr Survivr

How to Find Happiness in the Age of Hookup Apps

ANDREW LONDYN

Copyrights and Credits

Grindr Survivr: How to Find Happiness in Age of Hookup Apps by Andrew Londyn

© March 2017 by Andrew Londyn

All rights reserved under International and Pan-American Copyright Conventions. By payment of the required fees, the reader has been granted the non-exclusive, non-transferable right to access and read the text of this e-book on-screen. No part of this text may be reproduced, transmitted, downloaded, decompiled, reverse engineered, stored in or introduced into any information storage and retrieval system, in any form or by any means, whether electronic or mechanical, now known or hereinafter invented, without the express written permission of the author, except where permitted by law.

Kindle edition © March 2017

Print edition © April 2017

IBSN-13: 978-1545139561
IBSN-10: 1545139563

Photos of Drag Queen Vinegar Strokes used by permission.

Photo on page 164 used by permission.

Other images believed to be used under fair use or public domain for social commentary and criticism.

Contents

Preface: Congratulations! v

Introduction: Why Write a Book About Grindr? ix

PART I: THE PROBLEMS WITH GRINDR 1

    Chapter One: Welcome to Your Grindr Hell 3

    Chapter Two: Grindr Is Merely Technology 13

    Chapter Three: Grindr Is Making You Cheap 17

    Chapter Four: Grindr Makes Us More Superficial 23

    Chapter Five: Grindr Makes Us Nasty (Or More Tolerant of Nasty Behavior) 31

    Chapter Six: Is Hookup Culture Eating Away at Our Souls? ... 39

PART II: THE GRINDR COMMANDMENTS 51

    Introduction: Why We Need a Moral Code! 53

    Commandment I: Thou Shalt Not Be a Douche! 55

    Commandment II: Thou Shalt Take Responsibility (Blame Yo' Self!) 69

    Commandment III: Thou Shalt Not Seek Perfection (Someone Ugly Loves You!) 75

    Commandment IV: Know Thyself (Know What You're Committed To!) 89

    Commandment V: Thou Shalt Conversate! 103

    Commandment VI: Thou Shalt Not Be a Time Waster! 117

    Commandment VII: Thou Shalt Not Be Flakey (Flakey Men Are the Scum of the Earth!) 125

Commandment VIII: Thou Shalt Judge Actions, Not Words (I Hate Guys From "New Jersey"!) 139

Commandment IX: Thou Shalt Remain Joyful! 143

Commandment X: Thou Shalt Not Heed The Noise! 151

Commandment Summary: The Grindr Code: Live By it! 161

PART III: GENERAL TIPS, GUIDELINES, & RECOMMENDATIONS 167

Chapter One: How to Navigate the Tinder Trap 169

Chapter Two: Do You Look Like Your Photos? 183

Chapter Three: How to Spot Fake or Deceptive Profiles 193

Chapter Four: No More Coffee Dates (And Other First Date Tips) 205

Chapter Five: Bring Your Kinky Boots 211

Conclusion: This Book Works! 219

Preface: Congratulations!

So here's the good thing about buying this book and opening it up. By merely buying this book and beginning to read this, you are miles ahead of everyone else. That's not meant as flattery, but it's a simple truth. Most guys online aren't thinking critically about what they're doing or why they're behaving in a certain way. They just do the same thing over and over again, but they're expecting a different result. Well, guess what—that's the definition of insanity!

We log onto Grindr secretly hoping for a different result, but we get the same thing over and over again. You may have tried other apps—maybe Surge, Tinder or OK Cupid, and yet you're still single and frustrated.

Well, here's the good news: the fact that you took action says a lot about you. Most gay guys just go through the motions on Grindr over and over. You tried Grindr or other apps. Things didn't go so well, but rather than giving up, you went out and looked for a new tool to give you a new perspective. That's 50% of the battle right there!

A very wise woman once told me, "When people really want a change, they'll make it happen." A lot of people say they want a change, but their actions demonstrate that they're secretly quite content to keep doing the same thing over and over again. Alternatively, many gay guys may not even realize that there is a problem: they may find Grindr annoying at times or they may sense that something is "off" about the gay community, but their analysis never goes any further. But in this case, ignorance isn't bliss. You, the reader, recognize that something is not just a little wrong, but REALLY wrong with the way the gay community is now treating itself. You probably went to Amazon, read the reviews, and thought "I'll give this a shot." And that takes courage!

Keep that mentality throughout the book. I try to be funny and honest without being disrespectful, but at times, I'm going to propose and suggest radical things. These concepts might be uncomfortable or upsetting, but try to keep an open mind. Think of this book as an ugly coat in your favorite retail store. At first, it looks weird, and it's not your style at all. But maybe you try it on, look in the mirror and you discover that it makes you look like James Dean. Keep this attitude throughout the book. Don't read it passively. Yes, this book has a lot of tips and techniques, but I am also going to encourage you to do a lot of soul searching. And I can promise you that you will NOT like everything that you see. It's going to take balls to look at yourself critically, but you're going to do it anyway. You may be a sloppy bottom, but you've got more balls than the manliest top. And it's *that* type of mindset that makes you a cut above the rest.

So give yourself a pat on the back, because it's the only one you're going to get for a long time. This book, if read correctly, should feel like a roller coaster. So strap yourself in and don't be afraid to scream.

Part I of the book analyzes problems with Grindr and dating apps as I see them. You can't really change things unless you see the problem for what it really is. You have to see how they affect gay men as a community in order to find ways to fix the damage.

Part II is where I call my readers to live by a higher code. You can't force other gay men to grow up, but you can look in the mirror and start working on yourself. If enough people start changing, then that's when awesome things are possible. I'm not naïve enough to think that my book will exorcise every gay man's inner demons, but I'm hoping that spending half of the book looking at yourself will help you make better dating decisions and, hopefully, help you find happiness.

Part III is more general dating tips, recommendations, and observations. It's probably what you *thought* this book would be about. But as it doesn't involve working on yourself or helping the gay community, I put it last, knowing that my readers may not finish the whole thing. But if some critical thinking and self-reflection scare the crap out of you, feel free to return the book—or you can just read the sections designated as "tips." It's my commitment that all my readers get something of value from this book.

Introduction:
Why Write a Book About Grindr?

So you might be asking yourself, "Why would anyone write a book about Grindr? Maybe this guy is crazy or just wants to rant—or both." But the main reason I'm writing a book about Grindr and online dating is that the apps are fundamentally changing the gay community.

Gay life, as we have known it, is completely different from what it was just a few years ago. In some ways, change is good. Although there is still a lot of homophobia around the world, I think it's fair to say that by and large around America and Europe, homophobia has declined (at least somewhat) over the past twenty years. In many Western countries, gays now have non-discrimination laws and marriage equality. Again, there is still much more to do, but we have come a long way. So much so that gay teenagers and gays who are increasingly coming out don't see the need to go to gay clubs. Why segregate themselves when their friends are open and accepting (whereas 15 years ago they weren't)?

Remember that movie 21 Jump Street? A re-make of a 1980's cop TV show where Johnnie Depp got his big break. The movie starts with Jonah Hill, the loveable yet plump side-kick, recalling his days in high school around the year 2000. He was frequently bullied and called "faggot." But when he's forced to go undercover in a modern high school in 2012, he tries to playfully use the word "fag" to fit in with the "cool high-schoolers." They react with "OMG" and disapproval. Homophobic bullying is suddenly no longer cool; it's taboo. So let's champion progress where we can.

But on the flip side, as gays find more acceptance in the straight community, gay establishments such as bars and clubs no longer have a monopoly on gay customers. In fact, many of the gay bars are closing down. Recently, my local gay bar closed down, and I got a little choked up. At least half of all of my first dates took place at this one establishment. And all of a sudden, it was gone. More and more gay bars are just disappearing. And to those of us who "grew up" in terms of our gay identity going to them, it's a bit sad.

Of course, that's not to say that straight bars and clubs are booming while only the gay ones wither away. Straight people have their own dating apps and dating sites. And from a health perspective, more and more people are adopting healthy living that includes less drunken nights out, less smoking, and more Pilates, yoga, and weight training.

But the key difference between gays and straights is that before Grindr and the rise of apps, the gay club was the undisputed epicenter of gay life. Straight bars and clubs were never the epicenter of straight life. Straight men could meet straight women anywhere—at a bar, at university, at work, at a coffee shop. Because straight people are in the majority, effectively all establishments where socializing can occur are potential places to find a mate. And because society was far from welcoming to gay people, the primary place to meet gay guys was in a gay establishment. That's not to say that two gay guys couldn't look each other up and down and find each other in straight establishments, but there was always an element of "Is this guy really gay? If he's not, am I in danger?"

Gay bars and clubs were our only "safe space" for decades. And just so the PC police don't pull me over, let me say that I'm aware that gay clubs are not always safe spaces. Homophobic men can and do terrorize gay men by attacking gay clubs: the Pulse nightclub in Orlando is a prime example. But this doesn't detract from my broader point: by and large, gay men found solace and community primarily in gay clubs. And while that wasn't perfect, I think the "community" element was a good thing for gays.

"So why not just delete Grindr and other gay dating apps?"

I've been asked this question only once, so I take it most of my readers realize that this question is silly, but I'll endeavor to answer it nonetheless. With the rise of social acceptance and the demise of gay bars, gay apps are now the primary way of meeting potential boyfriends. Fewer and fewer people are going to clubs; that's why they're dying out. While fewer gays are going to clubs, the ones that do are primarily going to dance, not to scope out the talent. This is completely logical for a gay guy who's come out since the invention of Grindr. If you want sex or dates, you'll go to an app. If you want good music, you'll go to a club. Why mix the two?

Yes, you can join other gay organizations outside of gay clubs. I know gay sports clubs are somewhat popular, but let's be honest; most gay guys aren't keen on sports. And joining an organization such as a gay sports team or joining a gay book club like that takes a lot of energy and time. It's not a bad thing, mind you. In fact, I would encourage you to do it. Find a group of gay guys whom you can relate to on a level other than sex! That's missing in our community, and it's a great thing. But you can't deprive yourself of the majority of potential partners and expect a good result.

Whether you like it or not, Grindr (and other dating apps) are now the new epicenter of gay life or gay culture.

The vast majority of gay interactions you will have with new people will be online. Yes, you will always have your friends, and not all gay bars and clubs will close down. But now, with the ability to access hundreds (if not thousands) of gay guys online in a nearby area or a faraway land, apps are the new king of the hill.

When people asked the notorious bank robber, Willie Sutton, who had robbed over $2 million from various banks between 1920 and 1940, why he robbed banks, he quipped, "Because that's where the money is." Grindr is where the gays are, so we have to look at how we're behaving on these apps if we want to gain insight into ourselves and our community.

Back in the "Good Ole Days"

At the risk of sounding like your grandfather who's reminiscing about the 1940's, let's cast our eyes back in time. Back to a simpler time. A time before everyone had a smart phone. Back before Grindr dominated the gay scene. Let's cast our eyes far, far back…

To six years ago.

Maybe seven depending on how quick your city was to adapt to new technology. President Obama had just been elected, and everyone had hope. Cell phones were getting smaller and smaller, not bigger and bigger. You were still buying CD's, so Apple couldn't block you from transferring your music around between computers and iPods. Back in the pre-Grindr days, if you were single and wanted to meet someone (whether you were searching for Mr. Right or Mr. Right now), you had to go out to a gay bar or a club.

Yes, there were dating sites, but people didn't have camera phones and so you never knew if the photos were reliable. It was so easy to be catfished. Even if you wanted to get some decent photos online, you had to have a scanner or get a photo CD from the convenient store that developed pictures. And frankly, people who relied on online dating as their primary means of finding mates seemed a bit weird—as if they were pathetic or creepy. Why meet someone online and take all those risks when you could just meet them in the real world?

Back then, bars and clubs often had the same patrons. So you would get used to seeing the same faces. In fact, as a student, I counted on it. If you can think back to an even earlier time around 2003 before Facebook, you really couldn't keep track of people. You'd have a few good clubbing buddies, but sometimes you could even go out alone. Since the same people were always at the same bars and clubs, you could chance it, see some casual acquaintances while you were out, and hang with them. Usually, there was always an old man or two. (Not that they were that "old," but they were a little too old to be hanging out at the bar alone. I often found myself saying "if I'm that old and out at the bar by myself, I'll kill myself".).

Often if you were young and cute, the drag queens who usually ran or managed the gay bars and clubs would flirt with you or take you under their wing, or in many cases, they'd find you the drugs you were after. (I wasn't into that, but I had to keep it real.) The bar tenders might know your name or at least your face: usually, there was always one who'd pour you an extra strong drink—unless you live in England or Ireland where they're forbidden by law from doing that.) There'd always be someone to dance with, even if he wasn't your ideal type. In fact, I often noticed that if someone wasn't conventionally attractive, they'd often compensate by trying to be the social director of a large clique. It was like a gay version of Cheers!

I'm not saying that gay life pre-2009 or 2010 was ideal or perfect. There was plenty of promiscuity in the gay world before Grindr. But the "gay community" existed in a much stronger fashion than it does today.

The upside to that, relative to now, was that you were forced to interact with people who might not be "your type." No one dared walk around saying "no fats, no femmes, no blacks," because the manager of the gay club was a sassy black Drag Queen.

And because you had to interact with different people constantly and you had to interact with different people in order to make friends, you had more chances to meet a diverse group of people—both for dating and for general friendships. I'm not saying that gay cliques didn't happen. They were certainly there. But even the most exclusive cliques of the old days were more open and inclusive than they are today.

The great downside of clubbing back then, which I would later realize was a positive in disguise, was the relatively fewer number of dating options. I've always been a bit picky—or at least, that's what my slutty friends tell me. And even on a "good night out," I'd only see three or four guys that I thought were cute. After doing a few shots, I might get the courage to speak to one or two of them. Most of the time, they weren't that keen, but they were still nice to my face. Again, back in the old days, when people realized that they might see you on a regular basis, they weren't so vicious or rude when rejecting you. Today, people can be nasty online, because they know they won't have to see you or interact with you ever again.

Also, inevitably in gay clubs, people are going to drink, and more than once I went home with someone "wearing beer goggles." They seemed cute in the club, but the next morning, it was like…

But there were some positive aspects of beer goggles as well. If a guy wasn't super-hot, but merely average, I might give him a chance in a club if he had a nice personality, whereas I might never give him a chance on Grindr. Also, whoever you hooked up with (or merely just swapped numbers with), you'd probably take the risk of investing more time into them to get to know them, because going back out to the club, getting super drunk, getting the courage to chat to someone new required a lot of energy. Even in my early 20's, sometimes I'd hang out with a guy a few times even if he wasn't my idea of Mr. Perfect. My very first boyfriend ended up being just an average Joe that I just kept hanging around with. He was sweet but a bit of a drifter, no ambition, no drive. But we had fun and after six months, I asked him, "So does this mean we're boyfriends?" He replied, "Well, I haven't been sleeping with anyone else." And that was that: we were boyfriends.

Ah... How romantic!

In economics, they'd refer to this as "transaction costs." (Don't worry; this will be the only economics I bring up.) Transaction costs are the costs and expenses associated with getting into the market or field where you want to do business. So if you wanted to sell cars, you'd have either to buy them from somewhere else first or to build a factory to make them (in which case you would need to buy supplies) and then hire a work force to sell your final product. That requires a lot of money up front, just to compete for a chance to sell some cars.

In terms of gay dating, the transaction costs of finding a guy to date were dressing up, corralling a friend to go out with you, traveling to the dodgy side of town to get to the gay bar, buying enough drinks to get drunk, chatting someone up, asking for their number (or asking to go home with them), and then chatting to them the next day.... That makes me tired just thinking about it. It was never easy to find a good guy—unless you were super gorgeous (which most of us are not, despite what our mothers have told us). Because going to the club took so much effort, you'd have to think carefully before tossing a guy aside.

While gay guys lamented all of the drama associated with finding good guys, I now look back and think that the transaction costs had benefits. The community aspects of gay bars ensured that people acted more civil towards each other, because you'd never know whom you'd later need as a friend. The alcohol made you more open to chatting to someone who wasn't your ideal type.

And the trouble of finding a decent guy was enough to make you think twice before tossing the average Joe aside.

- A sense of community
- Interacting with different types of people—both for friendships and dating
- Having manners and being civil
- Dating people who may not be your ideal type
- Thinking long and hard before discarding someone

These are good things, and they're all but gone from the new Grindr age. So perhaps, this is just what happens with changing times, but if enough people decide that we want to collectively change things, then maybe we can work to reintroduce some of this into our community.

What This Book is NOT!

While I make no bones about urging the gay community to "do better" in terms of how we treat each other, this book is not a value judgment. I'm not going to get on a soapbox and try to tell you whom to date or with whom to have sex. Everyone has their own journey, and sometimes, when gays are new to the scene, they want to explore their sexual identity in various ways. But chances are if you're reading this book, then you've found that just sleeping with loads of guys for the hell of it isn't that fulfilling, and you secretly want something more substantial, but you don't think it's possible. What this book does aim to do is to break the cycle of cynicism that stops you and others from having a great relationship.

This book is NOT designed to convince you that heteronormative relationships are the ideal. Personally, I think monogamous relationships are beneficial, especially at the beginning of relationships, but you are free to choose for yourself. My longest relationship was four years, and it did NOT end well.

So who am I to judge a couple that has been together for ten years and now wants to explore other options to spice things up?

The problem is gay men don't have discussions about what types of relationships truly work for them. They kind of jump into new relationships, hoping that everything sorts itself out, but it doesn't work that way. The time to be thinking of what kind of relationship works for you is NOW while you're single. Critically thinking now about what kind of relationship you really need to be happy will make you more confident when you're considering dating another man long term; it will also help you more easily assess what type of guy is right for you.

People nowadays usually seek confirmation bias. They don't want to be exposed to new ideas or new thinking because that is upsetting. Take all the crazy people who watch Fox News all day. They're not interested in facts. They just want to be told what they already believe. And what's the result of that? President Trump.

The same can be said of all people—even liberal gays. There are some difficult truths we need to confront if we hope to grow as a community. So at times, I'm going to propose some controversial theories to get you to think. And guess what? Sometimes my theories may not apply to you. And that's okay. If you seriously took a moment to reflect on your behavior, even if you conclude that I'm wrong, then the book is working! So the goal of this book is not to convince you to agree with me 100% of the time. Personally, I'd love for you to recommend this book to others, but that's secondary. Your changing your life comes first! And that only comes from critical self-reflection. Feel free to question and doubt what I propose. Just begin to think critically about how your behavior impacts you yourself.

It's my goal to get a critical mass of young gay men who are willing to live by a certain moral code. I'll spell out this code later on in the book, but you don't have to adopt my code. You're free to create your own code. But whatever code you adopt, live from it powerfully! Know what works for you and what doesn't work for you. The point of this book is for you to choose your own path, rather than throwing your hands up in disgust and cynicism and just shagging mindlessly for forever.

About the Author

You may be wondering, "Who is this guy? Why would he write a book about Grindr? Who is he to give me recommendations on how to live my life?" If you must know, I'm a lawyer, and I've also dabbled in journalism. So I deal a lot with big egos and liars. I did my Doctor of Laws degree at Harvard, so I do know something about academia, although this book is not written in an academic form. So I'd like to think I'm someone who has spent a lot of time analyzing people and what makes them tick. I'm writing this book because I see very few people having these conversations about personal growth and development.

The other reason I'm writing this book is that I have been single for an incredibly long period of time, and I couldn't quite figure it out. I'm 5-11. I work out three or four times a week. I consider myself cute. I'm educated and have a career. In theory, I have a lot of good qualities that should make it easy for me to find a boyfriend. Prior to the new age of Grindr, I was never single for more than a few months. But at the time of writing this book, I had been single for about two years. Although I went on loads of first dates, it seems like finding a boyfriend had become nearly impossible. So I kept asking myself, "What the hell is going on?"

By the way, I freely admit that maybe it's me. Maybe I've unconsciously become what I hate about these apps. But at the very least, I wanted to explore the problems within myself and what I've seen in others, and hopefully, you'll find something valuable that applies to you.

This book started off as a blog: I was getting so pissed off by the way gay guys would treat me online that I needed to vent and get my thoughts out there. By writing things down, I felt better about things. But as people read my blog, I thought that maybe this book could be the beginning of something bigger: maybe my book could empower others to find substantial relationships that make them happy, or, alternatively, that they could powerfully choose to remain single without whining about how hard it is to find a man.

I'm not saying that everything that's wrong in the gay community is the fault of Grindr. Quite the opposite. The fault lies within the users, including me. I'm severely unhappy with the status quo, and someone has to say something about it. While I'm not the first gay guy to whine about what's happening to the gay community, I feel that my perspectives are different enough that I wanted to contribute to the conversations we were having in the gay community in a more meaningful way than just bitching to my friends and whining on a blog.

Part I:
The Problems With Grindr

Think about situations where people grow and learn: a self-help book, therapy, a personal development course, Alcoholics Anonymous—yeah, that's a more unusual situation yet very applicable. In all of these situations where people want to grow, develop and change, they must always confront the reality of the situation that they are in currently. They must see their circumstances for what they are, not what they want them to be. They must also take a critical look at their past and try to learn from their previous mistakes. So in order to navigate the new world of hook-up apps, you have to see the environment as it truly is.

Chapter One: Welcome to Your Grindr Hell

Ha-ha. Okay, maybe that chapter title is a bit hyperbolic. But it certainly feels that way some times when it comes to online dating. In the famous French play *No Exit*, author Jean-Paul Sartre depicts three people in Hell. They aren't tortured, but they are merely stuck in a living room together: a cowardly misogynist, a lesbian and a nymphomaniac are forced to get along together in this room for eternity. The lesbian has the hots for the nympho; the nympho has the hots for the man, but the man (while straight) hates all women. The climax of the play is the man's realization that *"Hell is other people."* It's not a fiery pit of torment; it's how we treat each other.

So it is in that spirit that I assert that gays have created a type of Hell on earth when it comes to dating apps. Perhaps, Sartre's characters could turn hell into a paradise if they dealt with their issues and learned to love each other. That may sound hokey, but the point is true. Grindr itself is not inherently evil. Grindr is merely a tool, a piece of technology. It's us, the users, who make it a terrible place to be. So that's why we must look at ourselves if we want these apps to produce better results.

The Vicious Cycle of Sluttiness and Cynicism

The greatest problem with Grindr and other apps is that there is a never-ending cycle of cynicism, and as gay men, we're spiraling further and further downward and out of control, seemingly powerless to break the cycle.[1]

We've all chatted to someone online and thought, "Oh, I'd marry him!" Maybe not marry, but maybe you were keen to get to know him or you really saw him as a potential boyfriend. But then that person doesn't respond, or he blocks you after one shag; he doesn't text back, or something bad like that happens. Inevitably, our feelings are hurt. Quite rightly we want to protect ourselves from getting hurt in the future, so little by little, we stop believing gay relationships are possible. We become more guarded, jaded, and cynical. Often, we just throw our hands up in disgust and think, "Well, if sex is all I can get, then I'm going to get mine." As our faith in gay relationships diminishes, we stop caring—about ourselves and others. We give in to base instincts over and over again. We know it's not fulfilling, but it's the only thing to do. So we spiral out of control.

Some people just feel hopeless or frustrated. Other people find themselves face down in a couch at a chem-sex party, getting done by random strangers, because they are so desperate to feel connected and accepted that drugs seem like the only way to have this experience. Again, I'm not judging, but we have to keep it real: too many gay guys are using drugs as substitute for acceptance and community. They're not happy with the situation but they keep doing it, because they feel hopeless, which in turn makes them often feel worse. But overall, I'd argue that the gay community is spiraling deeper into a cynical state, whether they use drugs or not. To paraphrase Michelle Visage: **"Getting filled" isn't the same thing as being fulfilled."**

I'd assert the spiraling descent goes something like this:

---

[1] Sometimes I refer to the vicious cycle as a "vicious spiral," since most people tend to spiral down into even more cynicism and sluttiness. So I use the terms interchangeably. They're the same thing.

> Level One: A New Hope
>> Logging onto the Apps with Lots Hope (re relationships) ➔ Bad Experience ➔ Hurt Feelings ➔ Using the Apps to Compensate for Hurt Feelings (w/ less hope than before, maybe hooking up with someone to compensate for hurt feelings)
>
> Level Two: Becoming Defensive
>> Logging onto the Apps with Cynicism ➔ Making Less Effort ➔ More Bad Experiences ➔ More Hurt Feelings & Disappointment ➔ Running Back to the Apps to Compensate

Grindr can become particularly seductive, for we crave the attention and the "quick fixes" it offers. We want to feel attractive. We want to feel desired. We think that one more hookup will wash away the bad experiences of the past, but it doesn't. Again, there is nothing wrong about having phases in your life where you want to explore your options and feel attractive. That's healthy and part of being human. The problem comes when you want to move past the hookups and onto something more meaningful. Given the current state of the gay community, Grindr interactions tend to push us down the cynical slut cycle more than we realize.

> Level Three: Giving Up
>> Logging onto the Apps Completely Cynical (now only looking for hook-ups) ➔ No Bad Experiences (b/c you're no longer trying) ➔ Getting the same result ➔ Feeling Hopeless Re Relationships ➔ Believing Nothing Substantial is Possible ➔ Using the App for Whatever Boost You Can Find

As we spiral downwards, we stop caring both about ourselves and our community, and that's when we create our own little app-inspired hell on earth.

As we're spiraling out of control, we become so cynical and switched off, we can't even recognize a genuine guy if he presents himself. Now another guy (maybe not your ideal type in terms of looks) views you as a real catch. But we're so caught up with our own cynicism, and we are so oblivious that we act like jerks because that's all we've experienced for so long.

We may know better, but we're rude, standoffish, or can't be bothered to expend any effort. So we subconsciously push away a would-be suitor, and we're not even aware of it. Or sometimes, when a guy wants to get committed, we freak out and act like total douchebags! In either case, we've hurt a good person, and pushed them onto their first step on the slow descent into the hell of cynicism and sluttiness.

> <u>Level Four: Blind to the Pain We Cause Others</u>
> Logging Onto Apps Completely Brain Dead ➜ Creating Bad Experiences for Other People ➜ Not Caring About the Consequences ➜ Missing Opportunities for Great Relationships But Not Realizing It ➜ Still Feeling Cynical ➜ Using the App to Compensate

Most people who act like jerks online probably aren't aware that they are behaving like this. No one thinks consciously, "I'm going to sabotage my dating life today, and I'm going to act like a dick to every sincere guy who is genuinely interested in getting to know me." As humans, we have a hard time seeing our bad side for what it is, so we wrap ourselves in "fig leaves" of excuses. "He wasn't my type at all." "What's the big deal? It's just an app." We may tell ourselves that we can delete the app at any time or that we will stop acting like a slut when we meet the perfect guy. But guess what? The perfect guy hasn't shown up. Or he might have presented himself, but we were too blind to see it. Meanwhile, now we're in bed with a crack-head, because we felt lonely and insecure at 3:00 in the morning.

So a big part of breaking the cycle is getting that YOU CONTRIBUTE TO THE PROBLEM! You may not realize it yet, but you do. Many people don't see the problem as emanating from their own behavior. They may feel that something is wrong, but they never bother to look deeper. They merely roam the gay app scene, looking for something new to consume, emotionally dead as a zombie. So I would take Sartre's words a bit farther. Hell is not just other people…

Hell is YOU!

Grindr: Where Sleeping Beauty Meets the Walking Dead

So yes, there certainly is a problem "out there" with the vicious cycle of sluttiness and cynicism. The online environment can be cruel, chaotic, or just laughable in its absurdity. Sometimes it's fun, but often it's just frustrating or disappointing. At times you've probably felt overwhelmed or hopeless. At times you may feel like you're drowning or at the very least, paddling upstream against a current of never-ending sluts and morons. But as much as you're annoyed with the situation "out there," there is an impact "in here," as in there's an impact on your own mind, heart, and soul.

"Not me," you're thinking. YES, EVEN YOU! "But I'm a nice guy. I don't mistreat anyone," you might say. Hmmm… Maybe… We've all been a douchebag to at least one nice guy. We had our reasons at the time, but we did something mean when the situation didn't call for it. But mean outbursts aside, your cynicism and beliefs that relationships aren't possible any more is the primary impact of the new gay world of Grindr.

"Yes, but it's not my fault that the guys out there are just dickheads," you say. That's very true. But your cynicism has weird ways of showing up. It bleeds into other areas, and you're not even aware of it. You may think you're this delightful, openhearted, warm, funny guy, and maybe your friends see it, and maybe your mom sees it. But to the rest of the gay world, you're either one of two things: dead or asleep. Hence the analogy: you're either a zombie (like in The Walking Dead) or a Sleeping Beauty, isolated and distant. There are only those two options if you're finding it difficult to find a boyfriend or a relationship of substance online in a large gay-friendly city.

"But I really want a boyfriend," you're protesting! Well, as I said in the Preface, the purpose of this book is to challenge you. You may not agree with everything I propose, but take time and consider it anyway. Try it on like a new outfit. See if it fits. It may not fit 100% of the people 100% of the time, but it will fit much more than you're thinking right now. With that being said... Welcome to your zombie apocalypse!

Mindless Shag Zombies

If you haven't seen the AMC TV show The Walking Dead, don't! It's terrible. Basically, a former police officer goes into a coma, wakes up, and finds that the zombie apocalypse has happened. Humans try to regroup and create small towns and villages, but ultimately, the zombies always break in and start eating people. It happens over and over again for seven seasons. Ugh. The zombies themselves crave human flesh and organs. They roam around the earth, searching for new, live people to consume. And no matter how many humans they eat, they never turn back alive. They're dead. They can't come back, and all that's left is the base desire to consume human flesh.

That's the majority of the gay community these days, and if it's not an outright majority, it's a pretty large chunk. The shagging zombies are those who have completely given up on the idea of a relationship. They may have tried it, gotten hurt, and decided it would never happen for them so why risk getting hurt again. And so they join the masses of shagging zombies on Grindr. Conversation is kept to a minimum because their brains have rotted from non-use. They just swap dick pics or ass pics and decide to consume each other's flesh. They've long stopped caring about whether the experience is fun or meaningful. They just do it because everyone else is doing it. They are constantly craving something more, a connection, but they are trapped in a mindless cycle that leads only to more craving and disappointment.

Any sort of effort to build a relationship outside of NSA (No Strings Attached hookups) is never expended. Only sex is offered, nothing more. Maybe if you're lucky, one of the shagging zombies will keep you around for a few shags, or they'll make you one of their friends. But a relationship with these guys is never possible.

Unlike the Walking Dead TV show, mindless sex zombies can come back to life! Eventually, they may get tired of roaming the planet looking for new penises to sit on or new butts to inseminate. But that's becoming less and less likely. What's far more likely is that they look for newer and weirder ways to get off with no strings. Gay guys jet around the globe, going to white parties, circuit parties, or chem-sex parties. But the result is the same. It's looking for new flesh to consume. And in a weird way, all of the remaining gay institutions are built around fostering more shagging, no connecting on an emotional level. Think about it.

What happens at gay clubs? People get drunk and hook up.

What happens on gay apps? People just hook up.

What happens at gay gyms? People stare at each other naked or sweaty in the gym and then hook up.

Gay bookshops, which at least had some semblance of community and fostering knowledge, are disappearing along with regular bookshops. It's another unfortunate side effect of technology.

We haven't used this technology to create new gay institutions that foster growth, friendships, or emotional connection without sex. If such exist, I can't find them. Maybe there's a gay couples retreat camp or something like that. But how many of those have you been to in your life? (I rest my case.) If we the people don't change, then we're all doomed to roam around like the walking dead.

Sleeping Beauty: Emotionally Dead Pretending to be Alive

Remember the fairy tale of Sleeping Beauty? Okay, if you didn't read Grimm's as a child, surely you saw the Disney version. Once she pricked her finger on the spinning wheel, she fell into a deep sleep—aka a coma. And she herself was unable to wake herself up. She had to lie there, sleeping, damn near dead, but still looking pretty. Her only hope was waiting for Prince Charming to ride in on a white horse, present himself as handsome and flawless, kiss her, and bring her back to life. ONLY THEN, Sleeping Beauty could arise from her slumber. She then got married and lived happily ever after. But until then, she's staying locked away in a tower, lifeless, unconscious.

Sleeping Beauties are gay guys who may or may not be slutty, but they are still emotionally distant, cut off, cynical, and effectively brain dead when it comes to relationships. But they spend a tremendous amount of time deluding themselves. Rather than take action and take risks, they give themselves feeble excuses, "Oh, I can't wait to find the perfect man! Then, we'll go off into the sunset and have a wonderful relationship." But until Mr. Perfect presents himself, Sleeping Beauties will NOT expend any energy getting to know someone. They don't initiate conversations or propose meeting for a date (unless the potential Prince Charming is way hotter than the Sleeping Beauty), and they NEVER do anything to risk getting hurt. And that includes doing anything that might make another guy feel special. So they play it safe, keeping their emotions hidden; they remain passive and effectively dead—fantasizing that Prince Charming will come along and rescue them from their helpless, hopeless state.

But the issue with Sleeping Beauties is that they're always looking for perfection. And if Prince Charming shows up, something WILL be wrong. They'll find a reason to shoot him down. Maybe he's not handsome enough. He's not "hung like a horse," or he doesn't make enough money. So he may not be Prince Charming, but when Clarence from Cleveland shows up, a Sleeping Beauty will overlook his good aspects and focus only on the negatives. Moreover, if Clarence hasn't succeeded in demonstrating his perfection to the Sleeping Beauties after two beers, he can forget it. Back to the tower they go! Or back onto Grindr rather. Then they lie dormant and wait for the next foolish suitor to present himself.

Sleeping Beauties often get on a moral high horse about dating and sex. They're quick to condemn the shagging zombies, but they're blissfully unaware that they, too, are stuck in the same cycle. They passively wait for someone else to present them with the perfect relationship, making Prince Charming do all the work as they delude themselves with their fantasy, "I'd walk barefoot into Hell for the man I truly loved." But they can't be bothered to re-schedule a date after they flake out.

Sleeping Beauties never question whether they need to adjust their dating criteria or grow as a person because they believe it's Prince Charming's job to prove he's worthy of their affection. Although they might decry a lack of good dating options, on one level, they're comfortable with the status quo. Always waiting for the perfect man gives them a fig leaf of a reason to reject anyone who doesn't instantly look or act like Prince Charming or who may require effort. And if they constantly have potential suitors supplied by Grindr and other apps, they never have an incentive to examine their own behavior and feelings. These bitches sit back and wait, but despite being hot, they're always single!

Slutty Sleepers

It's not as if being a mindless shag zombie or a Sleeping Beauty is mutually exclusive. There are loads of Slutty Sleepers who act like mindless shagging zombies, but they lie to themselves by pretending, "Yes, I'm slutty now, but I'll settle down some day in the future once I find the perfect guy. Once he's here, I'll happily commit to a monogamous relationship. But not today!"

Again, most Sleeping Beauties and Shagging Zombies don't realize what they're doing. They give themselves good excuses for acting the way they do. "I got hurt before, and I don't want to be hurt again, so I'll keep things casual." Or "He was nice, but maybe the next guy will be better." This type of attitude is commonplace among teenagers and people in their early 20s. But I know gay guys who have turned 35 and in all sincerity still wonder why they've never had a substantial relationship.

Are you starting to see yourself in this? These behavior patterns are the new normal in the age of Grindr. The problem is that fewer and fewer people make an effort to get to know someone and take risks on a potential boyfriend. And more and more guys focus only on looks and nothing else. This isn't a good mix for long term relationships! So more and more people give up hope and slide further down the spiral.

So we're left with a gay community where a large percentage is emotionally dead or passively waiting for someone else to "wake them up."

Some of you may be thinking "Jeez, that's depressing. What hope is there for us?" Well, there is hope. But first, we gay guys must start looking at our behavior patterns and start actively thinking and discussing these issues. If you're happy being a slut, keep doing what you're doing. But otherwise, you need to change yourself. You can't force a Sleeping Beauty to wake up or a shag zombie to come back alive. But you can certainly work on yourself. You can get smart about whom you pursue and in whom you invest your time. But first, you have to see objectively the state of the community that we're in. Frankly, relationship prospects on Grindr are grim and getting grimmer.

Chapter Two:
Grindr Is Merely Technology

Although I can get a bit preachy when expounding on the evils of Grindr and related apps, I want to be clear that I don't fault the Grindr app for what's happening to the gay community. Grindr is merely a technological tool. It brought together a number of things that were already happening. People were already going to bars less; and as the population adopted smart-phone technology, uploading selfies became easier. People are more comfortable meeting strangers online. Just like in No Exit, if the characters change themselves, hell turns into heaven. Grindr is the same way. Apps could unite the gay community in a way we never thought possible. That may be unlikely, but it's possible. It's all in how we use the technology. Imagine how useful Grindr would be if we needed to disseminate information quickly—potentially sharing new information and new treatments regarding HIV. Imagine how useful Grindr would be if someone who has yet to come out genuinely needed just a friend to talk to, to help them through a difficult time. Imagine how easy it would be if we only wanted to find a few local friends who shared common interests or wanted to hang out at the local bar or club. It's we who are making the app the new "dodgy bar" that self-respecting guys don't frequent, not the technology itself.

In addition to being a safe space for people who aren't out, Grindr is helpful for people who live in homophobic countries. If governments forbid gay establishments from opening, then people still in theory can find a safe space online. But sadly, governments like Russia and Iran have become knowledgeable of Grindr and have blocked the app in their countries. But again, it's merely a technological tool that brings people together faster than anything we've seen before, and it offers its users a multitude of choices. The problem is when confronted with these things, most users have turned Grindr into the world's largest receptacle of dickheads.

The Good Thing About Grindr

As much as I scream and cry about the horrors of Grindr, there is one upside to everyone treating each other like a gay Pokémon card. While everyone is becoming a superficial slut-zombie, the good news is that no one has the time or energy for mind games.

In the old days of five or six years ago when meeting guys was a bit harder, gay guys would attempt to hide their flaws because they didn't want their boyfriends seeing how crazy they really were. Gays were a bit more like straight people in that regard. Over a series of months, they would gradually let the façade slip off, revealing their full psycho selves, but it would take months, if not years, to figure this out. My longest relationship was four years, and I painfully found out that the man I loved didn't actually exist. He was a compulsive liar, who spoke lies and broke promises like a sociopath. And I'm not throwing that term out lightly. He told me I was his soul mate days before he ran off with another guy. It was one of the most emotionally difficult things I've confronted.

But I haven't had an event like that in all the time I've been single over the past few years. Yay, Grindr! A few have lied about their relationship status to get me into bed, but that's it. (That's not to say there aren't a million other ways that gay guys can't act like jerks, but no one is tricking or manipulating me.) At first I thought, "Well, no one's playing mind games because a guy has to be really keen to keep you first. And if no one's interested in anything more than a few shags, then no one has an incentive to manipulate you."

And I've been shocked at how willing people are to show their crazy side via text and on a first date. I was once on a first date with a guy, and he disclosed how he had to beat up his last boyfriend. Now, I am in no way making light of physical violence or domestic abuse, but he dropped that like it was nothing. What do you say to that? Honestly, how do you respond to that kind of statement? Needless to say, there wasn't a second date.

But this was the extreme. I've had loads of experiences where gay guys blocked me or went off on me for the tiniest little things. So I'm just inventing a theory here, and I can't say I've met enough psychos for it to be a statistically valid poll, but here goes: since there seem to be no immediate consequence for acting like a jerk online and gay guys have loads of dating options, people are growing more comfortable acting like jerks in real life. Also, the hotter you are, the more shit people will tolerate. So this "new generation" of gays has never had to train themselves in restraining their reactions or hiding their crazy.

The upside to that is that people show you who they are REALLY FAST. It's not that they can't help themselves, but that they've never even had to learn to try. So if they are obnoxious or vile, you will find out soon. This is the one good thing to come out of Grindr and online dating. Okay, that was a back-handed compliment to Grindr. And I can't deny the fact that Grindr has made it easier to find and meet people.

I once had a friend, Gloomy Grover, who begged me to take him to a new gay bar. Grover is very shy and has low self-esteem, despite the fact that he's very hot. Grover asked me to meet him at this new bar because he wanted to try to meet some guys in the real world. I was reluctant because the bar was on the other side of town, but Grover's a good friend, so I acquiesced. Of course, Grover was 20 minutes late. I was stuck standing in a bar, looking stupid all by myself. It was one of those bars where strangers look at you and cut you to shreds with a withering glance. I feared that I looked like the single guy who was *pretending* to wait for an imaginary friend to arrive, but who's just sad and pathetic. Either waiting for a tardy mate or desperately hoping a hot guy would walk into the bar happened to me a lot in the pre-Grindr days—and I don't miss those awkward waits or solo nights at all. Grindr and other apps help ensure you always have a date lined up rather than just waiting around and hoping someone new walks in. And let's be frank, nights out weren't very exciting the majority of the time anyway, so we can't say that the new Grindr age has been all bad.

And if you're visiting in a new town, Grindr is a great option to meet people and find out what's going on. Pre-Grindr, I can remember visiting new towns, reading about a certain gay bar online, and then arriving only to learn that it was the "wrong night" or the "wrong crowd." Now, if you're from out of town, you can go online and have a date waiting for you at the bar. So I won't pretend that Grindr hasn't given the gay community loads of new benefits. Just as new robots in factories made goods cheaper, they also cut the workforce, leaving many without a job or hope for economic advancement. There are always unintended human costs that arise from new technologies. But whereas losing a job is immediate and visible, the negative consequences from Grindr are long-term and hidden.

Chapter Three:
Grindr Is Making You Cheap

Grindr, as well as other apps, offers you far more choices and potential dating prospects than a traditional club. And the basic app is free to use; the Xtra version is only $8 a month—not even the price of one good cocktail. So if you're a poor student, it's a great way to meet people without having to use your student loan for a night out with mates. Anyone can use it for any purpose or to find any type of guy. These aren't inherently bad things; that's just the nature of technology. The internet gives us more options for a variety of activities outside of dating. But in cold economics terms, one of the reasons I believe Grindr is so successful is that it has eliminated ALL transaction costs that are associated with finding potential dates in gay clubs and bars. Grindr eliminates the costs, time, need, and risks of:

- Going clubbing and paying for club entry, drinks, and a taxi home

- Time to dress up and look cute to check out potential dates

- Liquid courage before approaching someone (if you do, then please close this book and get help immediately). And less drinking means fewer hangovers, which means you're more productive elsewhere in your life

- Persuading your friends to go out with you, since most people Grind alone

- Wasting entire evenings out only to find no cute guys in the club.

Grindr has certainly made gay life easier, and people aren't going to go back to the old way of doing things. But with all new technologies, there are trade-offs. We're losing our "community," the ability to hold a conversation face to face, getting to know people who aren't our ideal type (whether they're friends or lovers). But there is another effect when you eliminate transaction costs: **Grindr Makes You Cheap.**

It's making YOU cheap. It's making them cheap. It's making all of us cheap—or cheaper than we used to be relative to clubbing days. And it's not exactly as if gays were the most chaste people on the planet before Grindr. Because you had to invest time, energy, and potentially money, you'd think long and hard about discarding someone.

But now a hot guy can easily block you and find someone else in a matter of seconds. So what incentive do these guys have to invest time and energy in getting to know you? So even if you've resisted the urge to be a slut online, everyone else acting like one makes your job of finding a husband all the more difficult. For as you try to hold out and refrain from slutty behavior, everyone begins to look at you as if you're the crazy one: "Oh, you're after a relationship? You must be desperate."

Even if the "hot guy" starts out as being more relationship oriented, temptation has a way of changing that. As Chris Rock once said, "When sex chases me, I can't run that fast!" So if you're constantly tempted with sex, it's hard not to start down the pathway to sluttiness and cynicism. Whether we do this because we've been hurt and are becoming cynical, or we're just doing it because it's easy and everyone else is doing it, the result is the same: the gay online dating environment is shaping what we think is possible from gay relationships, and we adjust our behavior accordingly.

Our environments contribute to who we are; that's a simple truth. And although we don't realize it, Grindr and gay apps are an environment of sorts, albeit a virtual one. So as sex becomes cheaper, we're all affected. Even if you stay true to yourself and your own morals, fewer and fewer people view that as a positive.

And let's be honest, there are loads of guys who are so hot, if they asked you for NSA, you'd drop your pants in a heartbeat. We've all done it. And there is nothing inherently wrong with that. There's nothing wrong with jumping into bed with a hot guy. Sex is part of being human. But the problem comes when everyone is secretly wanting more than sex, but everyone is trapped in the vicious cycle and can't find anything else.

I can hear loads of you saying, "Well, I still meet guys for drinks from Grindr." Yes, absolutely. You can still meet guys who are up for drinks first. But the point is as our community becomes more focused on "cheap sex now," fewer guys are holding that same view.

Grindr Creates Lots of Competition

Even in a crowded club, once you were dancing with a cute guy, it was highly unlikely that someone else would come up to you and actively try to pull him away—though I have friends who do that. Guys may stare at the other guy, and maybe one guy would have the balls to say something to the hot guy if you briefly walked away to go to the bathroom, but by and large if you got the guy's attention, he'd be focused on you for at least fifteen minutes or the amount of time it takes him to down that cheap-ass vodka-coke you bought him. In that amount of time, you had a chance to see if you two clicked or if your killer personality made him laugh, or maybe he admired your confidence (even if you weren't his type).

Guys who were confident and had great personalities had the edge in clubs—at least in terms of pursuing the hot guys. But now people will send a message to a hot guy that they would never dare approach in real life. It's made it easier for everyone to approach that super-hot guy, and now they do. No one needs liquid courage or a great personality to strike up a conversation with the super-hot guy, so they take full advantage of this on apps.

The downside to this is that it makes it harder for you to hang on to a good guy—or at least one you think is hot. Increased competition makes it less likely that hot guys will want to settle down or date someone who doesn't look like their ideal type.

Nearly Unlimited Choice

"A man is basically as faithful as his options," Chris Rock said, referring to Bill Clinton. Again, it's true. For Bill Clinton, his charisma and lusts nearly ruined his presidency. Now, I think the impeachment was a travesty, but the broader point is accurate: too much choice can cause us to do stupid things that can damage us both personally and professionally. Just look at Hollywood celebrities. Is it really surprising that their relationships never last? Hollywood celebrities have loads of people trying to sleep with them, and eventually, all that choice causes people to cheat. And yes, I'm explicitly thinking of Brad Pitt: first Jennifer Anniston and now Angelina Jolie. (Hey… Angelina should have known that if they do it *for* you, they will do it *to* you.)

Well, the good thing about Grindr is that it makes hot guys local celebrities. They're inundated with choices, particularly if they live in a large city. And for those gays living in mega-cities like London, New York, San Francisco, and Los Angeles the choice can literally be unlimited (Maybe Paris, Berlin and Miami, but those have more tourists as opposed to new people constantly moving there.) These metropolises certainly offer better job opportunities than many of the small towns where we grew up, and many of us dreamed of moving to that "big gay scene" where finally we could be in a majority gay environment and feel "free" to be ourselves—at least, I did growing up in red state America.

A wide range of dating options is great if you have a "niche taste." Suppose you've just always had a thing for short redheads with ginger mustaches. Between Grindr and Tinder, honey, you can find ten in under an hour. Whatever your preference or whatever you're keen to explore, you don't have to wait around in the club, frustrated because your ideal type of guy isn't there that night. Hell, the dating app, Hornet, now lets you search for key words and phrases. So if you've got an interest that's really kinky or different, then you can find it online in a way you could never find in a club.

But nearly unlimited choice can also be overwhelming and confusing. I've had more dates in the past two or three years than I had in the rest of my life combined. That's entirely due to the options that you get from apps. And although I've had the most first dates over recent years, I would not classify them as my happiest in terms of satisfaction with dating. So don't get me wrong, I prefer more dating options to less. But with all new technologies that offer us more choices instantly, there are side effects, many of which we may not notice until it's too late.

Chapter Four:
Grindr Makes Us More Superficial

This is probably the understatement of the decade, but it's worth exploring. One of the reasons I had such a harder time finding a boyfriend over the past few years is that I became more superficial and didn't realize it. All of my life, I was skinny—like starving African child skinny. Well, starving children have swollen stomachs, so let's say I was rocking the heroin look without the heroin. I had gotten out of a four year relationship, and I was devastated. I thought this guy was "the one," and he turned out to be a complete sociopath—a compulsive liar like I've never encountered before or since. After giving this guy four years, I realized I wasn't really a twink anymore, so I joined a gym.

At first, I was lost in the gym. I had always hated sports as a kid, and I found the gym intimidating. But one day, my friend Andrew showed me his workout routine, where he only used dumbbells and barbells rather than machines. Within two months, my chest had a strong definition. I was still quite slim, but with some muscle growing. A few months later, however, I began dating a veterinarian, but by this point, I had been bitten by the gym bug, and I was constantly striving to make my body better; I was going to the gym at least four times a week, drinking protein shakes, reading articles about how to improve my workouts, and talking to personal trainers (hoping to get free advice). When things with the vet ended, I reemerged onto the new Grindr scene with a brand new body. And I loved it! As my pecs and other muscles grew, I only got more offers. A few super-hot guys even asked me out. It was amazing.

Suddenly, guys who would have been way out of my league a few years before were talking to me. And there's nothing worse than an awkward kid who turns hot later in life. I was always picky, but now I could be super-picky. I was still rejected by most of the gorgeous guys that I messaged online, but I still got a fair number of dates. Yet despite going on numerous first dates, none of them were clicking—or the ones I wanted weren't reciprocating. Getting a hot guy's attention became common, but holding onto it was impossible.

Suddenly something my sister once said to me as a kid hit me like a ton of bricks: ***pretty boys make bad boyfriends.*** Unlike me, my sister became remarkably pretty at a young age. She is almost 15 years older than I, but we have a very close relationship, and she's almost like a second mother to me. Because she was so pretty and had so many guys trying to date her, she would often make her boyfriends babysit me. (Yes, pretty girls can do that shit and get away with it!) So I met and interacted with most of them. As a six year old child, I gravitated towards the guy that was biggest kid himself. He was tall, handsome, and he liked cartoons, and he even bought me a few toys. (I have a feeling my sister put out after that.) But it probably wouldn't surprise you to learn that she didn't end up with the big kid. My sister ultimately married the guy who was less attractive but far more stable. Let's call him Stable Stanley. Stanley had been off and on with my sister for years. She played the field, but he was devoted. He was always there for her, and he was a true "friend." She once told me as a tween that she never felt that "spark of passion" for Stanley the way she did for others. But a few years later, out of the blue, they were engaged. Not understanding how a woman's biological clock starts ticking like a time bomb, I was perplexed. When I asked her about her sudden change of heart, she said, "Pretty boys make bad boyfriends." It took more than a decade for me to see the wisdom in those words. My problem was that I had become the pretty boy and didn't realize it.

I was smart, funny, and always had a larger than life personality—and I have a cute baby face. But people were never keen to be with me. Now, because I had muscles, the attention went to my head, and as a result I have done some shameful things. So I freely admit that part of my recent journey is getting over my own ego and insecurities. But the problem with apps such as Grindr is that they put ALL of the emphasis on appearance and none on personality or character.

Grindr gives you one photo for your profile. At least Hornet gives you four, and Tinder gives you six. So if you're going to be judged by that one photo, you better make sure it's a good one. And often people put a good photo up of somebody else! #Catfish!

In a club, you can approach a guy, and unless he's a complete jerk, you can usually chat him up for at least five minutes. He may ultimately shoot you down, but usually, manners would dictate that he chat to you for a little while, giving you an opportunity to let your personality shine. But now, that interaction will be decided upon one photo. All of the wonderful, interesting, quirky things that make up your heart and soul have no opportunity to shine on Grindr.

Profile Text Rarely Matters

Before, your profile text would appear over your main photo. So at least you had a chance or two to talk about yourself. But recently, Grindr has made the profile text appear on a separate page. You have to click down to see what a guy is about. And let's be honest, we usually make a split decision of "Yes, I want a piece of that" or "No way" instantly from their profile photo. We all do it. Yes, we may check the profile text later, but the profile text rarely makes a difference. And when it does, it's either to confirm what we wanted to see, "Ooh, the hot guy works at a law firm, so you know he's smart," or "Oh. That ugly guy works at McDonald's. What a loser. Block!" But if a guy is hot enough, you could switch job titles, and it wouldn't make a difference in terms of his appeal:

> "Ooh, that hot guy works at McDonald's. I want him to super-size it for me."
>
> Or
>
> "Yuck, that ugly guy is a lawyer. Who does he think he is? Pretentious twat."

In my experience, 95% of the time, profile text makes no difference at all. Text only makes a difference when you're really on the fence, thinking "maybe." But in my experience, the maybe usually turns into a no later, because you were never that keen to begin with.

When our entire potential interaction hinges on one photo, then how can this not make us superficial? I don't have any data to prove it, but I am certain that the rise of gays going to the gym corresponds with the rise of Grindr and app culture. You may have a wonderful personality, but nobody cares about that unless you have pecs.

That veterinarian I was dating used to decry all the superficial behavior of Grindr and apps while we were dating, yet as he saw my pecs growing, he got his skinny ass to the gym. He denied that the two were linked, but I saw right through it. He knew that as I became more attractive to a larger group of people, he needed to keep up. He possibly also felt a bit insecure about his body relative to mine. And it's the same principle with online dating.

I'm NOT saying that it should be this way. Trust me, I wish it were different, but for now, it's not. We're all becoming more focused on appearance.

I recently re-watched the original British *Queer as Folk*, and the hot guy, Stuart Jones, the big heartthrob player who always slept with loads of hot guys, was remarkably skinny for a guy in his 30s. Now I love the actor, Aidan Gillen who went on to star in *The Wire* and *Game of Thrones*, but as a sex symbol, I was like "Really? I'm not seeing it." But that's me speaking in 2016. I bet if I had been living in Manchester in the late 1990s, I would have let him use me for a one-night stand because that was the standard of attractiveness at the time.

If you're fortunate to have a pretty face or a hot body, the upside of Grindr is that you get to be Stuart Alan Jones—or Brian Kinney if you watched the U.S. version. In fact, you don't even have to be super-hot; you just have to be slightly cuter than most of the people in your local environment. The downside of apps making it easier to find potential dates means that lots of ordinary people get to feel like celebrities within their local communities. In addition to numerous dates, they can get followers on Instagram and Snap-chat. People constantly like and applaud every shirtless selfie (I'm guilty of that one), or even when they post stupid pictures of their food. But as with all new technologies, there are unintended consequences. And the result is massively over-inflated egos! Everyone thinks every picture they post should be hung in the Sistine Chapel. They think relationships either should be perfect and very easy (never requiring work or effort), or, alternatively, they have so many admirers, the notion of a relationship seems like a chore, so they can't be bothered. The bad boys from *Queer as Folk*—Stuart Jones (UK) and Brian Kinney (USA)—had strong, interesting personalities and good jobs to boot. That made them Alpha dogs in their group. They had confidence, and they were master pickup artists. Today, one only needs to look hot in photos—or merely "above average". No personality is required.

Grindr Is Killing Your Personality

Whereas your great personality might shine within five minutes of talking to someone in the real world, it's impossible to show this in an early online chat. There is NO way you can show your heart and soul to a guy in the first message. You just can't do it. If you try, you'll look crazy.

> *Hey. I'm a really sensitive, caring gay man, who's open, honest, and funny. I've also got a great educational background and a steady job. I'd love to chat to you and maybe meet you for a drink, because I thought you were really cute. I'm ultimately looking for a long-term relationship. How about you?*

First, they would think you were crazy. The typical stupid hot guy will read that message and perceive the following:

I'm a weak, sniveling coward. I'm looking for a relationship, because no one hits on me. I'll take ages to put out for you, and I want to tie you down and close off your other sexual options as soon as possible. And I'm listing my accomplishments in order to make you feel bad about yourself.

Ha-ha. Even if he may not think all of that so precisely, he might be like "Ewww. No chill" or see you as desperate. Trying to show your personality and positive attributes (not related to your appearance) is virtually impossible to do on Grindr. As a result, the smart people with great personalities are letting them go to waste.

Let's flip it around to examine the situation from the hot guy's perspective. If you get 50 guys messaging you every day, you're going to stop looking for anything on their profile that indicates that they have a good personality. You're just going to look at the guys who messaged you and respond to the hottest one. So the hot guy is letting his personality go to waste too. Personality is like a muscle: if you're not using it, then you're losing it. And now in app culture, a place where we in theory want to make meaningful connections with more people, there is no space to connect emotionally.

Yes, other apps give you more photos, and in having a few additional photos, you have more opportunities to show off the real you—or at least the "you" that you want potential dates to see at the beginning. (Deep down, you know you're more 2006 crazy Britney than 2001 peak stardom Britney, lol... Kidding! Don't arrest me PC police; I'm not making fun of mental health. Just making a joke.)

But at least on Hornet or Tinder you can show more of the real you. Usually people use their additional photos to show them in an exotic location. Oddly, lots of men (gay and straight) want to be photographed next to a tiger. I don't know why; it's not like they caught that tiger in the wild. That tiger is on more drugs than Drew Barrymore at grade school; you were in no real danger, honey. I'm not impressed.

But I admit that I do the same. I sometimes use a picture of me in Rome to show I'm well-traveled. I use a picture of me in a suit to show I'm intelligent and professional, and I sometimes use a picture of me at Harry Potter World to show I don't take myself too seriously. But the point is that we respond to visual stimulation, and the apps make this worse. You can try to send signals through additional photos that you're someone worth getting to know, but the sad truth is, your personality has little opportunity to shine in an initial online chat. Me going to Rome or me in a suit doesn't tell you whether I have a good heart or whether I'm fun to be around.

Grindr Did What No Bully Could: Kill the Gay Personality

Remember when the stereotype of gay guys was that they were incredibly funny, witty and charming. Straight women would always be envious of the fact that gay guys could speak so well, discuss a wide variety of topics, and be sensitive to other people's needs, while at the same time being hilarious and fun to be around. Often this over-exaggerated personality was a coping mechanism: if a gay guy were friendly with the girls, they would in turn stop him from getting his ass kicked. But the fact remains that gay guys in general tend to have cooler personalities than straight guys, in my opinion. But how many of you find your Grindr interactions to be full of humor and good conversation?

...

[Crickets chirp loudly as gay men sit in uncomfortable silence]

Yeah, I thought so...

This is just a theory, but I believe as society becomes more accepting, gays don't have to be as witty and quick on their feet to avoid an ass-kicking. And as sex gets cheaper, you no longer have to show your personality for a man to want to take you to his bed. The result is a generation of gay guys with no personalities. Again, at risk of sounding a bit like your granddad, I remember when most gays had personalities, even the hot ones! Now, fewer and fewer people have fun personalities. Again, I can't give you demonstrable proof that social acceptance and Grindr are making gays more boring as individuals. But a personality is a muscle like any other. If you don't develop it, it stays weak and withers. And if you have unlimited sexual partners and you don't even have to crack a good joke to charm any of them into bed, chances are your personality will stagnate.

Think about it this way: If having a great personality was key to getting hot guys into bed, Dr. Phil would never be able to leave the Bay Area. There'd be too much demand for his services! But we all know working on your pecs is going to get you more dates than working on your mind.

¯_(ツ)_/¯

From a different perspective, there is no negative consequence for having a flat personality as long as you have a hot photo. Why would you ever need to develop your personality if it will never affect your dating options? You may need a better personality to sustain a long-term relationship, but that's a relatively distant consequence, whereas getting dates on Grindr is an immediate reward.

Chapter Five:
Grindr Makes Us Nasty
(Or More Tolerant of Nasty Behavior)

In real life there's always a consequence for acting like an obnoxious dickhead. If you act like a dick to your friends, they will stop hanging out with you. And if you disrespect a stranger in public, you might just get your ass kicked, or at least get a drink thrown in your face. (I've done that more than once, but don't worry; it's always a clear liquid like vodka, gin, or Sprite—never red wine. Again, ruining a gay man's outfit is just wrong. No one deserves that.)

If you act like a dick on the job, you'll probably get fired—unless you're the boss, but even then people under you have a way of getting even: corporate sabotage, moving to rival companies, taking you to HR, or going to the newspapers when you run for president.

Of course, in Trump's case, acting like an obnoxious jerk got him to the White House. But I have a feeling Americans are going to look back in time with a severe sense of shame—at least I hope so anyway. I'm certainly not the first person to compare Trump's hateful rhetoric to obnoxious social media comments. In one sense, he's the embodiment of the new app age we live in. Everyone feels entitled to say whatever stupid thing pops into their head, and there are no consequences for saying dumb shit. Quite the opposite: we want to hear more dumb shit to make us feel less dumb. But to bring this back to gay men, do you really want a community that claims to oppose Donald Trump but acts just like him when no one is watching?

No Consequence for Bad Behavior Online

Trump aside, there are few consequences, if any, for acting like a jerk online. And most would agree that people now say things online that they would never say in real life. That's just a side effect of the cloak of anonymity that the Internet gives us all.

If you said something mean in a club, your friends might hear you and gasp, so you ran a risk that your community would react negatively. That drag queen might never let you back into the club again. Also, if you said something hurtful, you had at least to stand there and see the expression of pain and disappointment on another person's face.

Now, with a press of a button, you can make anyone go away, and you never have to live with the consequence of your hateful behavior. Don't get me wrong. Some people just keep messaging cock pics forever unless you block them, so we NEED the block button. But I am pointing out that one of the risks of such functions is that we are less present to how we impact others. We've become uncaring towards how our behavior harms other people. Yes, you can report abuse, and you should report it, but usually this by itself will have no consequence. Most apps will send offenders several warnings before banning them from the app. What's a warning from Grindr going to make an asshole do? Other than to bust out laughing!

And if your account gets deactivated, all you have to do is delete the app, reinstall, and use a different email address. So there are loads of ways of getting around acting like a jerk online. There's little consequence for acting like a douchebag.

Online Texting Leads to Real World Hurt

Grindr is merely a tool, and loads of unscrupulous individuals are happy to use it to manipulate others. I've met guys from Grindr who lied about their relationship status so they could use me to cheat on their boyfriends. I've also had the love of my life sneaking onto Grindr to find other men. I am even forced to admit that I've done that myself, and I'm ashamed to admit that. But downloading Grindr is easy to do, particularly when relationships are difficult or you discover that your boyfriend has cheated on you, so you think, "I'm going to get even with his ass."

But the bottom line is that Grindr and other dating apps give us more opportunities to do horrible things to people—both online and in real life. We can report someone for using abusive language on Grindr, but we can't report the guy who told you he'd meet you for a date then leaves you standing literally out in the cold for twenty minutes. And you can't report the gay guy who lied to you to get you into bed, and then blocked you once you've had sex because he wants to go back to his boyfriend.

I know—or at least I hope and pray—that you are now thinking, "I would never do that." I ask, "Are you sure?" Take a moment and think back to see if you've ever done something obnoxious to someone online. I'll give you a hint: you probably did it to someone you thought was ugly or not your type. But if that's still not you, then I say thank you! The gay community needs more people like you, but there's more that we can do. We need to be clear that we as a community don't tolerate intra-communal bullying or abuse. I'll get into the details of what we can do later, but for now, take a moment and think back to how you respond to people you find unattractive. It may not even be bullying. You may have flaked out on a date at the last second or stood someone up. But when you treat people without a basic sense of decency, you're telling the universe (be it karma, God, Buddha, or whoever) that you don't deserve respect either.

In one sense, Grindr is the Wild West of dating. No one has any incentive to be nice; there are no immediate consequences for acting like a jerk, and there is no enforcement mechanism to stop people from doing unethical things. We're the first generation to deal with this new age of dating, and so we're wondering around lost in a lawless desert—a desert abounding with the cacti of penis pictures, but void of nourishing water to quench our souls thirsty for real meaning. Part of our journey as the gay community, particularly for millennials, is charting out how people should behave online. Maybe everyone on Grindr should be forced to give the app the email of their HR manager. Then those bitches wouldn't be so vicious. But short of that, I'm not sure there is any way to force moral behavior on amoral users. We can, however, do more to let others know we won't commit or tolerate abuse.

Think about the long-term consequences if we do nothing. Gays under 25 have no experience of the "good old days" when the gay community was more solid and coherent. All they will know is Grindr and online dating. If there's no moral code to at least act as a guide for younger gays, then in fifteen or twenty years, we're going to be left with a community of Donald Trumps. Now ask yourself: are you okay with that? So we gays need to think about the moral development of the twinks—not just about shagging them!

Fewer are Willing to Invest Time & Take Risks

I once took a seminar on relationships, and one of the homework assignments was to do something romantic for someone else. That assignment was kind of scary because I was single with no solid boyfriend prospects. I had met a cute guy on Tinder. He was an aspiring architect, so let's call him Arnold the Architect. But unfortunately, Arnold was only visiting from out of town. He seemed like a safe bet, I thought, because if it backfired, then none of my friends would be able to witness my humiliation. *So what do you do that's romantic for a guy who lives thousands of miles away?*

I sent him flowers, and I made a Power-point presentation. Trust me, the power-point presentation worked. It wasn't a business analysis full of pie charts. I created a presentation that listed all of the reasons I thought he was special—great smile, volunteering with disabled children, smart, and more stuff like that. And then I synced it to his favorite song. It was more like a mini-movie than a power-point. It was a real risk, because the last time I sent flowers to a guy who wasn't my boyfriend, he made fun of me on Twitter. (I can't tell you how devastating that was. See my chapter on I Hate Guys From New Jersey.) But the assignment worked, far better than I had hoped. Rather than viewing me as an afterthought, Arnold took two vacations to come visit me, and he even applied for jobs in my area. Ultimately, he didn't get the jobs, and we didn't end up together, but the assignment taught me a lot about myself. Also, in doing the assignment (ordering the flowers, compiling the power-point, and learning how to sync it to music), I got invested in hoping things worked out with Arnold. I viewed him as a cut above the rest rather than just another guy on a list.

If you want love and a relationship that lasts longer than the time it takes the two of you to cum, you have to be willing to take risks and invest some time. This seems totally obvious in theory, but it's petrifying in practice. When we put effort into people, we feel invested in them. So we're less likely to throw them away on a whim. But due to Grindr and other apps that require little effort to find a potential date or shag, you never feel invested in any one person. And if you're never invested in just one person, then you'll never value them or treat them with respect. You devalue them to a mere photo and a few lines of text.

App culture makes everyone completely fungible and easily replaced. With a push of a button and a few lines of text, you can be replaced, and a potential mate can find someone just like you. Yes, and I mean just like YOU! If you're a twink, a bear, or a muscle Mary, any big city is going to have multiple people who look just like you. And since we all just judge each other by photos, there's no way for you to distinguish yourself.

Think of it this way, why should your dream man (that you see on Grindr) invest his time into you? I can hear a hundred gay guys saying simultaneously, but "I'm special. I have such a big heart and I'm so caring, blah, blah, blah...." Everyone thinks they're special. So why should your dream man invest time into *you*? Why should he invest in you, when he can find ten other guys who look like you? What separates you from the rest?

This isn't rhetorical. Take a few seconds and think about what makes you special to a potential boyfriend.

(It would be so cool if I could insert the Jeopardy theme right here... Or the Countdown theme if you're British)

Oh wait... As most of you are probably reading this in e-book format, I'll post the links:

Remember take a few seconds and think about yourself.

Jeopardy:

https://www.youtube.com/watch?v=vXGhvoekY44

Countdown:

https://www.youtube.com/watch?v=M2dhD9zR6hk

I'm sure you used the 30 second theme song to meditate deeply and discover enlightenment. Yeah, right. Well, a lot of gays are narcissistic, so thinking about yourself should be fun. So what did you come up with?

I have a feeling that the qualities you're thinking of are INTERNAL, and they can't be easily displayed in your Grindr photo or in the initial conversation. Good guys don't have a chance to showcase their best qualities. The technology gives us lots of choices, but in turn, we become more picky and less willing to take chances on investing in a virtual stranger—unless they are super-hot and "out of our league."

But there are always major risks when you take a gamble on a guy you don't know that well. One set of flowers got me a guy flying thousands of miles and looking for jobs in my area. But another set of flowers got me an abusive rant on Twitter.[2] I'll discuss some strategies when deciding how to take big risks. I

---

[2] For the details, Go to Commandment VIII: I Hate Guys From "New Jersey."

can't promise that you'll never get hurt. But I can ask you to think about the impact on the gay community.

- What impact does making people fungible have on us?
- How do we value ourselves?
- What's the impact on your life outside of dating if you never are willing to make the first move or take risks in relationships?
- If no one is willing to invest their time online, then what are the long-term consequences?

Again, I don't have easy answers, but I'm 100% convinced that there is an impact, and on balance, that impact makes it harder to build strong healthy relationships in all areas of our lives.

We Look For Reasons to Cross Someone Off

In the good old days of six or seven years ago, if you found a good guy in a club, even if he weren't "perfect," you'd hang on to him for at least a few weeks, because finding someone "better" required a lot of time and energy, so you'd hang on to your average Joe for a while—or in my case 18 months. **Now, in the age of Grindr, we have so many options, many of whom are quite keen to pursue us, that we now look for reasons to discard the Average Joe, long before we've assessed whether he has anything to offer on the boyfriend front, because we need to hurry up and get to the next guy who's asking us out for a drink (or showing us his cock).** The wide range of choices motivates us to kill off anything that doesn't look like "perfection." As a result, we're closed off from a lot of amazing possibilities.

You may assume that this was merely an issue for me, but if I'm wrong in my assertions about the gay community, why aren't more men finding the love of their lives and getting married? All of my evidence from observing myself and my friends shows that gay relationships are becoming more difficult to find and harder to maintain than they were in the past. Even though it seems counter-intuitive, our abundance of choices is sabotaging our ability to connect with people. It's just too easy to bail at the first sign of trouble and find someone new. Or we have so many dating choices that we're so keen to meet (or shag) as many of them as possible that we're just not in the right space mentally to find a good boyfriend. There's little incentive to invest in one individual when you have ten others knocking at your door. Our relationships, like paper plates, plastic forks, and take-out meals, have succumbed to our throw-away society.

Chapter Six:
Is Hookup Culture Eating Away at Our Souls?

One of my friends once told me, "Random sex is like eating fast food. Once in a while, it's okay, but doing it all the time makes you feel sick." I laughed at this because it rings true for a lot of people. I'm not judging us men for being slutty. We're all guys; we all have needs. And there are plenty of religious zealots who will condemn us and try to deny us basic rights based solely on whom we love. But by eliminating all of the transaction costs to gay dating, and making it easier to hook up, are we losing something as a community? Are Grindr and other apps pandering to our baser instincts and thereby hindering our development as adults? Does online dating today hurt our ability to have long term relationships later in life? Does hookup culture corrode our souls?

Given the scope of what I've just proposed, I can't answer this question with absolute certainty. My experience is limited to me; your experience is limited to you. But there are a lot of hard questions that we as gay men aren't asking. This was an issue before Grindr, but I fear Grindr has made the problem ten times worse.

Again, there are phases in life where it's healthy to explore your sexuality with regards to relationships. Straight people start doing this at age 12, maybe earlier. They hold hands, give each other pecks on the cheek, and give themselves relationship titles of boyfriend and girlfriend, even though the relationship ends after a few days (although I'd hope they're not having sex at that age). They also use these formative years to figure out what kinds of girls they find attractive, what they look for in a dating partner, and they begin dealing with the pain of breakups and rejection.

So while straight people have had their adolescence to come to terms with their raging hormones and these difficult issues, most gays don't deal with these challenges until they're in their late teens or early twenties. Some don't acknowledge their sexual identity until much later in life when they've had a wife and kids. So there's a time to keep things casual, but I humbly ask my readers:

Does promiscuous behavior really make you happy?

Does it really make you feel fulfilled (particularly once it's all over and done)? For myself, the answer is no. I don't sense from my gay friends that they are happy with the status quo either. And by buying this book, you've demonstrated that the online dating scene isn't working as well as you'd like. (And even if someone bought you this book as a gift, your friend got it for you because they were tired of hearing you whine about not being able to find a nice guy.) So maybe we can agree that there is room to grow beyond the slutty-cynical cycle, and yet how do we do this?

Being sexually intimate with someone is a way of investing in them. (Some of you are giggling right now because I said "invest in someone.") There's a reason the word "intimacy" often is used interchangeably with words denoting sexual relations. Again, I'm not saying that meaningless sex doesn't exist or that it doesn't have a role at times. But sleeping with someone carries a value or significance that is hard to articulate in a short paragraph. Most readers probably hold the belief that sex, while not always meaningful, is a significant bonding activity unlike other activities.

So if we're hooking up with anyone and everyone, what value are we assigning to the people we sleep with? Are we dehumanizing others in the process? Are we dehumanizing or devaluing ourselves? Again, I don't know the right balance for every individual. I'm just asking people to ponder the questions. Maybe gay structures—both clubs and apps—cause us to act in a way that feels good in the moment but can be damaging to our long-term mental health.

When I was first drafting this book, I went back home, and I hooked up with a very cute twink. We had a date, but his personality didn't knock me over, but I slept with him anyway—just because he was hot. First, the sex was a bit awkward because he was a tad short, and we didn't know each other's bodies. And we did it in the dark, so I couldn't even enjoy his pretty face.

After it was over, I just wanted to go home. Right before I left his place, he leaned in and kissed me on the cheek. I can't explain why he did it, but it was almost as if he did it because he was expected to do something before sending a one-night stand away into the cold. (Maybe it was a goodbye kiss because he lived in the ghetto. :-P) As I was walking back to my car, feeling weird and empty, I suddenly thought, "Wait a minute. I got exactly what I wanted. The hot guy said yes! You're living the dream." And yet I wasn't fulfilled at all. "Why did I do that?" I kept asking myself. While I was thankful that I hadn't been rejected, I was far from happy.

Now, I'm totally responsible for my own behavior. Grindr didn't make me shag that cute twink. But somehow, I felt like I had let the environment of Grindr compromise my standards. And afterwards, I felt worse than before. The sex didn't feel natural. It didn't germinate organically from a fun-filled evening and a genuine connection. It felt forced and awkward. I could tell by the way he kissed me that he intended never to speak to me again. I wish I could define it more clearly. But sometimes, you can just tell that from the look in a guy's eyes or his body language, and that made me feel weird. I drove home with an uneasy feeling. I was only visiting for a few days, so why did I even care?

So when I got home, I waited an hour. I sent him a text, thanking for the fun time. And of course, he didn't respond, but it was late. So I went on to Grindr just to see when he last checked in, and he was there ONLINE—not there 55 minutes ago, but online currently! WTF? Is he that slutty that he needs to find someone else at 3:30 in the morning? Moreover, why did I (with all of my alleged wisdom and insights) just let a slut use me like that? I'm supposed to be better at weeding out bad ones? Now that it's all over, what was the point? We're not friends, and we're never going to speak again, so what was this all for?"

To make matters worse, to compensate for the feelings of emptiness inside of me, I started messaging other guys, and by this point it's 4:00 am, so the caliber of man likely to be awake and online is quite dodgy. I knew chatting to other guys wouldn't help, but I did it anyway. Don't worry, I didn't do anything more than chat. But suddenly I was desperate to find someone else to at least tell me I'm attractive, in order to make up for the slutty guy who found me attractive but not enough to text back.

I'm responsible for my own behavior and actions. I took a chance by hooking up with this guy. And I freely admit to overanalyzing everything. But that instance brought home my own entrapment in the vicious cycle of sluttiness and cynicism. I knew my behavior wasn't in keeping with my usual standards, and I felt empty afterwards. The boy didn't lie to me or mislead me in any way. He didn't even promise to text again. He just gave me that weird kiss. But I somehow felt rejected, even though I was only visiting, and I had, from the outset, relegated him to being worth no more than a one-time shag. I should have been feeling triumphant, but I didn't. And foolishly, knowing better, I threw myself back into the apps to try to make things better, but that never works!

Sex should be fun, and it should be empowering in a way. You can try stuff that you later may not choose to repeat, but if you leave a sexual encounter feeling worse than before, something is wrong. Again, I can't blame Grindr for this mistake, but I think app culture is a bit like the Shoulder Devil that pops up on TV whenever a character is in a moral conundrum. It can influence you, but it can't force you to do anything. But where's the Shoulder Angel to balance you out? Gay culture and app culture are constantly tempting us, but from where do we get our moral guidance? Like many cartoon characters, we may swat the

Shoulder Angel away, but at least, we need to hear something, some voice encouraging us to be better than what we are.

Do You Secretly Like C**k Pics with Your Cheerios?

So if I asked you individually, "Do you really want to see a cock pic with your breakfast?" most of you would say, "No, it's gross." And yet it happens. I've asked myself, "Why am I on Grindr?" Everyone on it seems to be sleazy. The "good ones" don't respond, and if they do, it never goes anywhere. So why the hell am I wasting my time? Particularly since loads of unattractive people send me loads of dick and ass pics.

I was having this conversation with one of my friends, and he gave me a very honest assessment: "I like looking at guys' cocks." Well, at least someone's honest. But I don't think that's true for everyone.

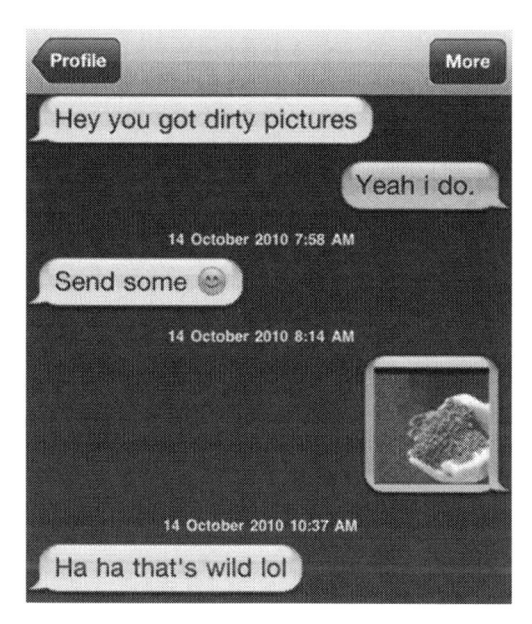

Not too long ago, I was chatting to a guy and asked him to send me some additional photos. I specifically requested normal ones, not nudes. Well, you guessed it. He sent the cock pic anyway!

Shocking! I asked him why he did that, and he told me that he felt like he needed to do that to keep my attention, because he didn't think he could get my attention otherwise. What happened after that was more disappointing. When I tried to engage him in a conversation, he got annoyed and blocked me. So he sent me a cock pic because he felt that was the only way to get my attention, but when I tried to relate to him as something more than his anatomy, he got annoyed and cut off the conversation.

Think about that for a minute. He was so committed to just having no-strings-attached fun, the notion of chatting with me first occurred to him as so much effort that he'd rather just block and move on to the next guy. First, I could write a whole essay on what might have been motivating this guy, but one thing is simple: he didn't want me to relate to him as anything more than his cock.

Maybe in that moment, he just really wanted a shag. I can't blame him for that. But it does make me pause and reflect as to how he might value himself. Contrary to what I think sometimes, people are rational actors—at least within the confines of their own personal journey and what they find acceptable. In short, if guys are sending cock pics all the time, someone is responding positively to it. If sending cock pics didn't get them laid, then they would eventually stop.

This takes me back to my original question. I'm not going to lie: most of the time when people do that, I roll my eyes. But every once-in-a-while, if the cock is attached to an attractive guy, I'm like "Hello!" Even if I don't respond or decide to take things forward, I like the ego boost in that moment: a hot guy wants to shag me, and that feels nice.

That momentary ego boost caused me to look at myself on a slightly deeper level. Even if most of the cock pics that come at me are gross, I do like the affirmation of people finding me attractive. And whenever I sign onto Grindr and have no messages, I'm disappointed. Whenever I hear that distinct Grindr buzz (indicating I've got messages), I light up, even if I know there is a 99.99% chance I won't find them attractive.

So to take it back to "Why am I on a stupid app like Grindr?" I came to a negative conclusion. I hardly get any real dates from Grindr. Most of mine come from Tinder. But I waste way more time on Grindr than all of the other apps combined. Why? Because I enjoy the ego boost of strangers trying to hook up with me. The ego boost is satisfying enough for me to keep wasting time on that skanky app. Tinder messages are far less frequent; that's most likely because you can't message everyone on Tinder and because I've chosen not to match with people who would do anything to get my attention.

So are we as gay men addicted to ego boosts? And I'm not saying that I'm a crack head, wishing each moment that someone sends me pictures of their junk, but how you spend your time says something about your character. And if I spend more time on Grindr—all the while resenting the app for not giving me what I say I want, then I've not taken a close look at myself. I always thought of myself as very confident. In fact, numerous people have told me that I'm arrogant. But if I enjoy people throwing themselves at me online, then maybe I'm not as confident as I believe. A truly confident man doesn't need to mess with that nonsense to prove his worth.

So I'm now forced to ask myself: If I know this weird dynamic is occurring, and I don't do anything about it, and I keep coming back to the same app, then do I secretly enjoy receiving dirty pics? Yeah, I may not want NSA, but I still crave the attention.

Important Update from MTV Australia

This chapter started out as a blog post, but I recently found a fascinating interview where a guy on MTV Australia seemingly nailed the issue for the entire millennial generation. In short, he said that social media (and you could argue the media in a wider sense) has made life seem easy. Even if we're depressed, we know how to "add a filter" and make everything look great. He also pointed out that when we get "likes" on Facebook and Instagram, we get a hit of dopamine, a chemical in our brain that makes us feel good. The hit of dopamine gets addictive, and so we crave it more and more.

He also pointed out that the millennial generation doesn't know how to form deep meaningful relationships. Everything is about instant gratification, but in life, a great online presence can't give you job satisfaction or deep relationships. Those can only be achieved the old fashioned way, and these new online tools may not be equipping young people to create that. If you want to watch the entire speech, I highly recommend it:

https://www.facebook.com/MTVAUSTRALIA/videos/10154938261678993/.

Or if you just Google "MTV Australia sums up millennial," it comes right up.

THANK GOD! It's not just gay people! Whew! [Massive exhale of relief]

But just to check, I googled "dopamine and social media," and there was no shortage of articles that reinforced this point.

http://www.theatlantic.com/health/archive/2012/07/exploiting-the-neuroscience-of-internet-addiction/259820/.

https://www.psychologytoday.com/blog/brain-wise/201209/why-were-all-addicted-texts-twitter-and-google.

https://www.cnet.com/news/this-is-what-social-media-is-doing-to-your-brain/.

In a sense, Grindr is just Facebook or Instagram on steroids. Rather than people liking our photos, they want to have sex with us. That's a far more primal instinct, and so it might be bringing out our primordial responses. It also explains why we (myself included) spend more time on Grindr, even though we know it won't give us anything substantial. So we might all be Grindr Addicts and not know it. Even if we're not totally addicted to Grindr and going online, we love the little ego boost we get. So, again, I ask, "Do you secretly like cock pics with your Cheerios?" And if we're becoming emotionally addicted to trivial things such as cock pics and Instagram followers, what's the impact on our hearts and minds? We can't pretend that there is no effect.

Every Gay Man Needs a Wife and Kids

While I'm not advocating any one thing to force onto gay behavior, I look at straight institutions, and I see how the structures of that society reinforce monogamy and long-term relationships. Along with that comes emotional connection and personal growth, which I find lacking in the gay community. Again, I don't judge, but I am forced to ask whether our hookup culture has "gone too far." Maybe we've thrown the baby (strong relationships) out with the bathwater of religious hatred and intolerance.

Not to stereotype 50% of the world's population, but as a general trend, I think most women prefer monogamy and stability over random hookups. They certainly do relative to men. That's not to say women can't be sexually liberated or slutty, but I think once that biological clock starts ticking, they want to settle down, and they're not shy about demanding this from men. Keep in mind, my sister was mistreated by her fair share of "hot" guys before she decided she wanted to marry her Stable Stanley. And when she changed her tune, she wanted marriage ASAP! She was the embodiment of Beyoncé's phrase: *If you liked it, then you shoulda' put a ring on it.* She got her ring!

Gays will get on the dance floor, imitate Beyoncé and copy her hand motions, but we're doing it while we're getting drunk and looking for hookups. We may know the lyrics verbatim, but we're not hearing what Beyoncé is saying. The single ladies still prefer the stability of a relationship, but the man's fear of commitment forced them to come to terms and embrace being single.

The other "structure" of straight society that forces people to "grow up" is children. Once a couple has their own child, their lives change; it's all about the baby or the kids. Anything that's not aligned with ensuring the healthy development of the children is no longer a priority. It's happened with all of my straight friends, save one! All of my best girl friends from high school and college won't return texts or invite me to hang out anymore.

While I'm disappointed, I accept that they have new priorities. And they weren't going to be any more fun anyways, because new moms are too exhausted to go clubbing. And fathers know that when the baby comes, they MUST provide. "Good men" take care of their kids. "Bad men" are deadbeats or are serial philanderers. Religion, TV, books, everything in straight society emphasizes this point.

That's not to say that straight men don't act promiscuously when they can get away with it; they certainly do. And I'm not blind to the fact that 50% of marriages end in divorce. So while I accept that not every gay man will want to have children or get married, I'm arguing that there is some value in getting involved with something that forces you to grow up, primarily by focusing your attention on someone else or a larger cause than merely yourself and your next shag. A wife and children force this on straight men, but what about gays?

Most gays are screaming, "My job!" But our careers are ultimately designed to enhance and enrich us. If we are successful, we earn more money, and the focus remains on us. I'm not saying that gays must have children to grow up or do charity work to be less self-centered. But as I'm looking around at the gay community and the gay things that tend to unite us as a group, I just don't see much that forwards our moral development. And I repeat, this does NOT mean that straight men are morally superior to gay men. But the average straight man is going to be confronted with more situations that force him to grow up than a gay man with a similar background and socio-economic status.

Where is our "put a ring on it" champion? Where is that moment when we get super clear about our long term commitments, and we have an "Ah Ha" moment where we realize that acting childishly and obnoxiously (whether it's online or in the real world) is ultimately unfulfilling over the long term? Neither Grindr nor the gay club scene encourages this type of introspection, but I do think Grindr is making it harder to grow as a community, and I wish more gay leaders would do more to prod our moral consciences. We're very good at giving lectures to straight people on how they need to be more tolerant or accepting of us, but we don't seem to be as adept at holding up a mirror to our own behavior as a community of adult men so that we stop mistreating each other.

Again, I'm not throwing shade here. For too long gays have been so persecuted from the outside that getting government leaders and communities to accept us has rightly been our top priority. But now that we're starting to gain social acceptance, what do we do with all the freedoms and acceptance we've achieved? There are still other forms of homophobia that need to be fought. But just because we have been or might still be oppressed doesn't mean we get a pass to treat each other like shit.

I see thousands (if not tens of thousands) of gay guys living in a large city, all shagging like rabbits, but wondering why they can't they get a boyfriend or find anything more meaningful.

With no external forces encouraging us to think critically about our dating priorities, we continue on, trapped in our self-centered spiral of cynicism and sluttiness. In general, straight men will experience pressure to grow out of this mentality as women push them to get married and have children. But there is no such pressure on gay guys. So with no pressure to change, will we ever?

Back in the old days (this is probably further back than ten years), once a gay guy found that he couldn't get laid as easily as he used to, due in part to being in his 30s or 40s, he'd wise up and start to settle down. But now, with the wider dating pool on Grindr and other apps, working out at the gym, Botox to stop your skin from wrinkling, and some extra money for a nicely furnished shag pad, which is easier to have when you don't have to provide for children, gay men can continue to act like teenagers well into their 40s or beyond. Some older gay men use drugs and chem-sex parties to lure hot guys over; once everyone is on drugs, no one cares about superficial qualities, and everyone wants to shag even more.

Some straight men might view this and think gays are lucky. But as a community, I don't believe that we're satisfied with the status quo. Not everyone is going to agree with me here, but it's something I feel strongly about. And your having bought this book means you sense that something is wrong, or, at least, needs improvement.

Precious few forums exist to make us question our actions, our thoughts, our priorities, so we stay trapped in the same cycle, which means our dating life consists of one word messages, dick pics at breakfast, and easy shags with strangers, followed by never speaking to the person again. Yes, this book will have tips and techniques on navigating online dating, but you as a reader can't control the people that message you online. You can control how you behave and how you treat people. You can begin to look inside yourself, confront hard truths and begin to grow accordingly. And *that's* what this book aims to do.

Part II:
The Grindr Commandments

Introduction: Why We Need a Moral Code!

Commandment I: Thou Shalt Not Be a Douche!

Commandment II: Thou Shalt Take Responsibility (Blame Yo' Self!)

Commandment III: Thou Shalt Not Seek Perfection (Someone Ugly Loves You!)

Commandment IV: Thou Shalt Know Thyself, (Know What You're Committed To!)

Commandment V: Thou Shalt Conversate!

Commandment VI: Thou Shalt Not Be a Time Waster!

Commandment VII: Thou Shalt Not Be Flakey (Flakey Men Are the Scum of the Earth!)

Commandment VIII: Thou Shalt Judge By Actions, Not Words (I Hate Guys From "New Jersey"!)

Commandment IX: Thou Shalt Remain Joyful!

Commandment X: Thou Shalt Not Heed the Noise!

Summary: The Grindr Code: Live By it!

Introduction:
Why We Need a Moral Code!

I'm not religious. But there is some value to religion in that it gives human beings a forum to debate morality and question how we should treat each other. The problem with gay guys is that because religion has by and large abused us, we have just stopped having these types of moral conversations. As a result, we've thrown the baby out with the bathwater. And while organized religion may not work for most gay men, we still need a forum to debate morality and personal growth.

The risk is that gays are becoming increasingly amoral. That's not to be confused with immoral. Amoral means without morals. Immoral means having bad morals. I'm referring to the "I don't care" attitude perpetuated by Grindr and other apps, which is making us all blasé about how we treat each other. Quite rightly, we don't need someone telling us that we're going to hell for being gay, but maybe we need someone prodding us to question ourselves and pushing us to grow as human beings and as a community. And I'm not saying that the straight community isn't dealing with the same thing. Quite the opposite. But the difference is that relying on apps is not the epicenter of "straight life" if such a thing exists. Apps are now the center of gay life. And if they are here to stay, "Now what?" How do we confront and transform the new world we find ourselves in. The next section will deal with basic dating tips and recommendations for navigating the apps, but remember, it takes two to tango. If you want to stop being a Mindless Shagging Zombie or a Sleeping Beauty, then you've got to deal with yourself.

I've been waiting for years for Lady Gaga, Elton John—or maybe Karen Walker from Will and Grace—to come down from a mountain top and declare that gays have a new set of commandments to which we should all adhere. But alas, it hasn't happened.

I admit that I hesitate to proscribe or prescribe morality to another human being. Who am I to propose guidelines for human behavior? I'm nobody important. Yes, I'm smart; I'm a lawyer. I have a background in philosophy and examining how humans behave. But I'm not ballsy enough to say that God sent me here on a mission. And I don't have any celebrity status to bolster my claims.

I'm just a normal guy who is out there trying to get people thinking, and if my ideas have merit, then perhaps people will reflect on them and find what's applicable to their own lives. I hope that as I share my ideas, other people will engage in these types of conversations, and people will develop their own internal code or commandments by which they will live. So these are my recommendations for gay men living in the new world of apps, but feel free to comment, criticize, change or adapt them to fit yourself. My main purpose is that you THINK about how you behave online, reflect on how that behavior affects you in the "real world," and start getting the results that truly make you happy.

That being said *Gay Recommendations* or *Gay Reflections* is nowhere near as catchy as *Gay Commandments*. So here we go. Back up, bitches. I got this shit! Just call me Grindr Moses!

Commandment I:
Thou Shalt Not Be a Douche!

This is the most obvious. You're likely thinking, "Well, of course." Yet it's the one that is at greatest risk for being violated, for as gays are overwhelmed with choice, online manners go out the window. As people get more and more messages on Grindr and other apps (i.e., they're hot and lots of people fancy them), they just give up caring about how they act or how they treat people. And as no consequence comes from acting like a shithead online, people just continue to do it.

Most of us can think of one time that we were a douchebag to someone for no reason. Maybe we were having a bad day. Maybe we thought the guy messaging us was "not being realistic." Being attractive is a form of power. And in typical corny geek fashion, I'm going to quote Spider-Man: "With great power comes great responsibility."

Own it. You have the power to hurt people. You have the power to ruin their day or make them sad. Yes, it's only Grindr. And yes, people shouldn't take rejection personally. But you have no idea what the person on the other side of the app is feeling. You have no idea what they've been through or where they are in their own journey of self-acceptance. Now honestly, do you want to be the type of person who uses your attractiveness to hurt people who took time to try to get to know you?

By the way, if a bunch of excuses are jumping into your head right now giving you reasons to ignore this advice, then ***that's how you know you're a douche!*** Stop making excuses and start recognizing other people's humanity.

I once messaged a guy on Grindr, and he responded with a Simon Cowell meme:

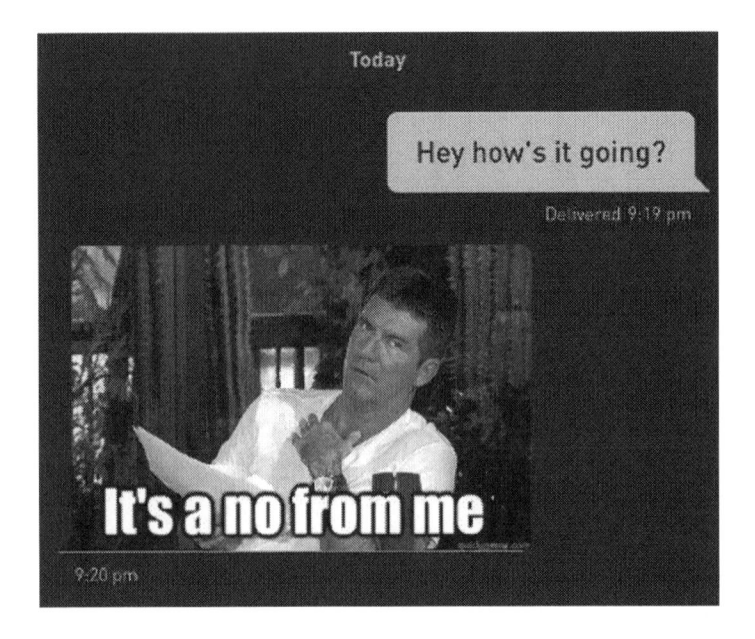

Keep in mind, I got this meme BEFORE I had muscles. And looking back now with several years' distance, it is kind of funny. But at the time, it was hurtful. Here I am, a Harvard lawyer with a cute face. I've just broken up with a sociopathic boyfriend, and I just wanted to meet a new guy to date, and he sends that.

That type of mentality is the epitome of the douchebag virus that's permeating all of Western culture, but it's a particularly acute problem in the gay community. Gay guys often revel in rejecting another person. And that's wrong! That's sick. When we tear down each other, we're no better than what the right-wing preachers say we are: in fact, we're worse. Evangelicals don't know any better; they're just following their interpretation of a righteousness code from the Bible. But gay guys should know better because they've already experienced discrimination. I sense little compassion in the gay community for men who aren't viewed as sexually attractive. And that needs to change before our community can truly flourish.

It's in your own self-interest to treat people with respect. You never know when and if you will bump into those same people in the real world. They may be in a position to help or hurt you when you need it the most. You may have forgotten them, but they won't have forgotten you and your vicious attack.

Personally, I always ignore or block people. I don't make them go through the "false hope" of seeing that they've received a response from a guy only for it to be dashed with a message like "Thanks but you're not my type." Trust me. That two second roller coaster sucks. And let's be honest: guys who send those message, whether they admit it or not, are secretly getting off on rejecting other people.

And for God's sake, do not tell them *why* you don't fancy them. I'm shocked at how rude gay guys are. It's bad enough to send someone a message saying, "Not interested, sorry." But don't tell them off because they're not pretty enough or don't have a muscular physique. And certainly don't abuse people or put them down because of their race or ethnicity. This goes without saying, but I'm shocked at how easily people just say horrible things on Grindr and other apps. Again, if you went around saying those things out loud six or seven years ago, you'd probably get banned from all the good clubs. Now people just emit casual racist comments like Donald Trump.

You may not think this type of attitude will come back to haunt you, but it has strange side effects. In 2008, the state of California put the question of whether to allow gay marriage to a referendum. (That's a horrible idea, but they did it.) There was cause for optimism. California is liberal, and Obama was on the ballot. Well, Obama won the state, but gay marriage still failed. Gay rights leaders analyzed the results and found that African-Americans and Latinos voted for Obama in overwhelming numbers and then turned right around and killed gay marriage. When they surveyed their gay colleagues of color to ask why more wasn't done to reach out to communities of color to promote marriage equality, they were confronted with a nasty truth. Many gay people of color felt discriminated against by the white gay community. They never felt supported or accepted. So they had fewer incentives to "come out" and bring awareness and education to their communities. And that lack of awareness killed gay marriage, albeit temporarily—thanks to those who fought for justice through the courts.

Without undervaluing the wonderful activists and campaigners who worked tirelessly to achieve marriage equality, we must also acknowledge that in one sense we got lucky because we had a president in the White House whose very existence was defined by creating dialog and understanding between different communities. Obama used his power to promote marriage equality, and many gays are about to see what it's like when the guy in charge doesn't care about your community. So while you might have a particular sexual preference, don't use it to hurt other people. Don't torment or disempower others. It costs nothing to be the bigger person online or to show some grace when you have to let someone down.

Here's a hint for whether you're acting like a douchebag: if you'd be embarrassed for your work colleagues or your mom to see what you wrote, you've probably already crossed over into douchebag territory.

I can hear some of you thinking, "Well, I might act a certain way online, but I'd never do that in real life." But your behavior online is part of your real life. In a sense, that is your true self—when you think no one is looking. So ask yourself: if you spend hours a day acting like a jerk online, treating people with disrespect (and demonstrating your own cheapness in the process), and as you are keeping that behavior pattern in place over weeks, months, and years, are you really saying that these thoughts and actions won't influence you when you are off line—in the "real world"? Not even a little bit?

A successful American businessman once said:

Watch your thoughts, they become words;
Watch your words, they become actions;

Watch your actions, they become habits;

Watch your habits, they become character;

Watch your character, for it becomes your destiny.

The quote is sometimes attributed to Margaret Thatcher, for Meryl Streep made the line famous in the film *The Iron Lady*. Indian revolutionary Gandhi said something similar:

The thought manifests as the word,

The word manifests as the deed,

The deed develops into habit,

And the habit hardens into character.

So watch the thought and its way with care,

And let it spring from love

Born out of concern for all beings.

The point is that acting like a douchebag online will take a toll on you. Whether you realize it or not, that kind of negativity will seep into other areas of your life. Moreover, we as a community need to do more to combat online abuse of all kinds.

By now, you may be thinking, "Straight people do this too." Yes, of course, and I'm not saying they're right or more moral than gay people. The key difference is that Grindr is now the epicenter of the gay community. We all need to be careful about how we treat people online, whether we're gay or straight. But straight people, by virtue of comprising over 90% of the population, have other ways to meet and interact. Gays need to take responsibility for how we treat people online and off line— because we are more likely to use dating apps than straight people, and because gays are a persecuted minority, we should demonstrate more empathy and compassion than others.

We all may lose our temper from time to time and say something we regret. But better that we're working on it and minimizing those mistakes than actively encouraging them.

The Douchebag Tests

Test 1:   If People Are Telling You that You're a Dick, You Probably Are!

Most people reading this section of the book may think that it applies to others "out there," but not to themselves. No one wants to think of himself as a bad person, but none of us is perfect either. We all have room to grow, and there is wisdom in reflecting on the impressions of others who have tried to get close to you.

To keep with the Simon Cowell analogy, if you keep auditioning for talent shows, and everyone says, "You can't sing," then maybe you can't sing. That doesn't mean you can't change. That doesn't mean you don't love music or connect with it profoundly. But maybe, your ass can't carry a tune. So if people are consistently telling you that you're behaving terribly in the field of dating, then maybe there is something to consider.

Analyze the last few times that people have told you that you were an asshole, a jerk, a douchebag, or a disgusting human being—whether online, in person, or via phone or text.

- How recent were these incidents?
- Do they happen frequently?

If it's happened more than twice in the last few months, then congratulations! You've got the douchebag virus! (But don't worry; it's easier to cure than herpes.)

A douchebag's first response will be to get defensive and make excuses. "They don't know me. There are two sides to every story. My mom thinks I'm great." But actually, if you're consistently leaving people with the impression that you're a terrible person, maybe, just maybe, you need to allow for the possibility that your behavior needs to improve. Stop resisting and just answer the two questions. Try this on like a new coat in a store you wouldn't normally frequent. It may seem hideous at first, but keep the coat on by keeping an open mind.

Yes, people lash out when they've been rejected or when you don't respond to their cock pic. But I'm not talking about that. I'm talking about hearing the feedback from people **you** led on for months, gave false hopes to, stood up, or flaked out on. So if in the last three months, more than two people have told you off for bad behavior, then you probably have a problem. None of us is perfect; we all have our issues. At least you're willing to consider yours.

Test 2: The 'Tell Your Girlfriend" Challenge

Part of my hypothesis about bad online behavior is that we're becoming amoral because we see no consequence for our behavior. If we were confronted with the real impact of our bad behavior, then we wouldn't act that way. So I've invented a way to test whether we're being a real douchebag. But keep in mind, this second part is not as easy as it seems. In fact, every single person I've proposed this to has not had the balls to try it.

A) **Find someone who will talk straight with you**. This might be your sister, your best girlfriend, your best gay friend, but make sure that it's someone who will be completely honest and call you out when you're out of line.

B) **Flip the Script:** Describe the situation that led to someone accusing you of being a "douche," BUT... **Reverse the roles!** Describe the situation to your friend as if you were the victim of the offensive behavior. Make it appear as if bad things were done to you, not by you. Do this and see how your friends react. It's quite revealing.

So if you were supposed to meet a guy for a date, and then you canceled on him because you just didn't feel like missing an episode of Glee that evening, then switch it around. Say to your friend:

> Girl, I was supposed to meet this guy for a drink, but he told me he'd rather stay home and watch TV. He canceled on me at the last minute. What do you think?

The key here is to be totally honest with your friend and include the details in your description. This will help you see yourself as you really are, and it will help develop some compassion for what you put the other guy through. So suppose you lied to the guy as you were flaking out at the last minute. You told him that you had a friend in the hospital when secretly you just wanted to stay home and watch TV. Tell that to your friend!

> Girl, this guy said he had a sick friend in the hospital and that's why he needed to cancel our date with no notice, but I saw on Twitter/Instagram that he was talking about staying home and watching Glee. What do you think?

You may have to add something to your story to explain that you knew they were lying. Obviously, you knew you were lying when you canceled the date. So your friend needs to know about the lie also. Be real with yourself and your mate, and watch what happens.

C) **Observe and Learn.** When your friend thinks that her gay bestie's been hurt, she will have strong words, condemning the behavior. Good! Gays need more of that if we're going to change how we behave online. And if her reaction is something like "Oh my God, what a shithead," then congratulations, **YOU ARE A DOUCHEBAG!**

Friends have a way of trying to defend us, even if we're wrong, because they want to be loyal. So most people won't tell you the truth if you fess up to why you're acting like a douche. But in reversing the situation, you can get a really good grasp of how the other person feels. And that's what's missing with online dating. No one takes any time to develop sympathy for people we casually hurt. But if we switch the roles as we tell our friends the true facts of what happened, we'll become aware of the impact that our behavior has on other people.

Once I went on a date with a model from New Jersey (he wasn't really from Jersey, but that's my code word that I will explain later). He was beautiful. We had a nice first date. At first he said he wanted to meet up again, but then he stopped texting. Rather than just letting go, I followed up and asked him about it. He told me that I said a few things that came across as snooty and condescending towards models. I felt terrible. I thought I was being funny, as he laughed the entire time, but I wasn't sensitive to how I was coming across. So in order to try to make amends (and get a second date), I sent the guy flowers. Yes, it was silly, but he was super-hot. And I was looking for a way to show that I wasn't a prick.

But after the flowers were delivered, I heard nothing. No "thanks but no thanks" text. And certainly nothing along the lines of "Oh how sweet. Yeah, let's meet up again." I didn't know what to do, so I thought I'd look him up on social media. There on his Twitter account was a picture of the flowers I sent and a caption that read "Nice flowers but dream on." Again, he didn't send that to me. He just decided to deride my gesture to all of his friends.

To date, that is the most horrible thing a gay man has ever done to me (if you subtract my sociopathic ex). Luckily, he didn't have my Twitter name, but that was one of the worst feelings I have ever had. Needless to say, I was livid, and I told him off. But in a manner that has become all too commonplace, he saw nothing wrong in doing this. He had no regrets and no sympathy for my pain or humiliation. I was floored by his callousness. He did it with such ease that it disgusted me. So I suggested he switch the roles and describe it to one of his friends and see how they reacted. He, of course, didn't do it. But on some level, I know that he knows that if he went to one of his friends and said, "Hey Girl. I sent this guy flowers and he made fun of me on Twitter," she would be shocked and appalled. She'd probably offer to "Cash Me Ousside! How-Bow Dah," thinking she was taking up for her friend. But it was the Jersey model who was the douchebag. This

Commandment I 63

model had zero compassion for the hurt caused by his nasty, disgusting behavior. And that infuriated me. That embodies what's wrong with gay society these days. And without some sort of mechanism (or test), gay guys are never going to learn or grow.

You may not be as vile as the Jersey model, but we've all done something careless without thinking, and it's had devastating consequences for others. I'm not saying that you have to write to Oprah for absolution every time you want to block a guy on Grindr for repeatedly sending cock pics to you during breakfast. But I guarantee there are times in your past where you've unintentionally hurt someone who was genuine and open to something meaningful. And you probably were shocked when he told you off. So that's why we need the douchebag test. Any practice that helps you stop doing that will ultimately help you. If Prince Charming ever arrives, you don't want to push him away by acting like a narcissistic jerk.

D) **Apologize!** A big part of making a relationship work is seeing how your behavior unwittingly hurt your partner, seeing things from his perspective and then apologizing while making amends. If you don't know how to apologize, you will NOT have any long, meaningful relationships in the future. You may be hot, but you're not *that hot*. Eventually, Prince Charming will get tired of the narcissistic attitude. Train the muscle now before it's too late!

Apologizing is always scary, because you won't know how the other person will react. He may be skeptical or angry. Don't let that stop you. ***Deliver an honest and sincere apology, explaining how you've realized how your behavior probably hurt him.***

E) **Let Him Vent.** And if the guy is still angry after you apologize, deal with it! Man up! Take five minutes and listen to how you hurt this guy's feelings.

If you can take a dick, you can take some criticism.

Be gracious, even if they're not. That's healing for them when they get to tell you how they really feel. Give them the opportunity to vent and ask follow up questions. Yes, it might be awkward, but if it's all via text, you have nothing to really fear. And if it gives them some closure, then it's worth it. Your five minutes of tolerating their reaction may make a world of difference for them. Since you didn't want them, why not endure a few minutes of awkward conversation so they can heal and find someone who will love their crazy ugly asses just the way they are.

Think of this as practice for Prince Charming. You can run and hide by blocking the guy you hurt, but that's not a character trait that will serve you well when real conflicts inevitably arise during a long-term relationship. At the very least, you will develop your empathy towards another human being, and that's what our community needs more of.

My Own Douchebag Impulses

I rarely start a fight, but I do know how to finish it. My biggest flaw is that when I get angry, I turn into a monster who will say anything to score a point. And by not catching myself in the heat of the moment, I've pushed away some great people.

I once had a date with a very sweet guy named Peter; he was a teaching assistant. His career hadn't really taken off, as he was still living with his parents, but he had a sweet heart. We had an amazing conversation where we talked philosophy, religion's impact on gays, really high-minded stuff that often doesn't come up on a first date. This was super attractive to me, as it was a welcome change from the boring chats that go nowhere. So we started kissing, but I noticed that Peter was a bit pudgy—far more than what his profile photos had suggested.

Now, had I been in the right state of mind, I would have just told myself, "You met a great guy, get over it." But I was newly single, my muscles were then toning and growing, and that opened me up to more dating options. I didn't want to be a complete jerk and refuse to date him, but at the same time, fitness is important to me. So I naively thought, "Maybe I can change him." So in my stupidity, I asked him if he had considered working out, and I offered to show him my gym routine.

Needless to say, the results weren't pretty. He saw right through what I was implying, and he became furious. He started cursing me out. He was really upset. He actually started going off on me about my intelligence and career choices. During our first date, I opened up to him about how I didn't get my dream job a few years back and how it haunted me every day. (I came close to working for someone very famous, but I was eliminated in the final round.) Peter told me, "That guy dodged a bullet in not hiring you."

Okay... I can handle you calling me a superficial cunt. But aiming for my career while rubbing my lost dream job in my face was a punch below the belt. I suddenly saw red. It was as if I grew fangs. I instantly lunged for his jugular. I ripped into him in a way that would make Anne Rice blush.

I told him off, threw some below the belt punches myself, and then blocked him in order to ensure that I got the last word. But once it was over, the anger faded. And I suddenly asked myself, "Well, what was that about? Do you feel better now?" No, I felt worse. I felt guilty for attacking a guy about his appearance. I looked like a complete ass. And I had punished a boy whose only crime was liking me too much (and not going to the gym). I made an enemy out of a great human being. I've dated a lot of guys, but very few of them were as wise and deep as this guy. Guilt started seeping in. I tried to dismiss it, but I couldn't escape the realization that I acted like a total douchebag. Part of me loves to win an argument, but I've never reveled in hurting other people for no good reason, and that's what I did. Although I tried to continue on dating vapid models and pretty boys, I would still think about Peter on occasion.

So a few months later, I took an old spare phone (because we had both blocked each other from texting), and I wrote out a long apology text. I sent it off. At first he said, "Who is this?" But suddenly experiencing cowardice, I didn't reply. (That was very weak of me). But he quickly deduced who it was. He said, "Thanks Andrew," and he said he appreciated the apology. And that was that. That was about three years ago, and I have never seen Peter on any other dating app in all that time. Perhaps, he moved away. Or perhaps, someone saw how great he was and snatched him up, and he's been happily committed ever since. I wish Peter well, and I know it was my loss. But at least I made the effort. He was gracious to me when I apologized. Most guys probably will be. Most of them will probably have forgotten you, but you should still apologize and hear them out if they're angry.

I'm not saying you have to invite in your stalker for a cup of tea. But if you can think of areas where you know you did something slimy, under-handed, shady, mean, rude, outrageous to someone who was kind and genuine, then bite the bullet and apologize.

Maybe you didn't tear into him the way I did with Peter, but you said something mean and hurtful. Maybe it was an off-hand remark that was biting. Or maybe you said nothing, ignoring him when he was making a good effort. Or maybe you flaked out on someone or stood them up. Take five minutes to see. You know you did *something*, so take a few minutes and email or text them an apology, or at least an explanation if you mysteriously stopped calling or flaked out.

Commandment II:
Thou Shalt Take Responsibility
(Blame Yo' Self!)

So if you're like me, then you live in a large city with a big gay scene, and yet everyone sits around annoyed that they can never find anything substantial or make a relationship last more than a couple of shags. (This commandment may not apply to everyone, but it certainly applies to anyone living in a large Western city)

Here's the truth: you probably did meet the right guy; you were just too blind to see it! You were either being a Sleeping Beauty or Mindless Shagging Zombie. Yes, you may have had a nasty experience with a New Jersey model (like I did), but not every gay guy is like that. It's too easy to become bitter, throw up your hands in disgust, and just give in to the vicious cycle. But there's no power from being a victim.

Like most gay guys, I'm a Democrat. I think Republicans are racist, homophobic, and just plain nasty. But when Herman Cain (the black CEO turned presidential candidate) said, "Don't blame Wall Street, Blame yo' self," I cracked up. It still makes me laugh now.

Here's the quick excerpt I'm paraphrasing:

https://www.youtube.com/watch?v=SHMEC8Xk9cg.

The one thing where I can sympathize with Republican aims is around the field of personal responsibility. I'm not saying that average folks should be blaming themselves for the near global financial collapse of 2008. But a great place where you can "blame yo'self" is in your own dating life, especially if you live in a Western country that has gay rights and you live in a city with a fairly large gay population. So brace yourself for another "ugly coat moment."

Even if your bad luck in dating doesn't seem like your fault, you're still responsible for it!

I can already hear you saying, "But it's not my fault I haven't met the right guy! I've had my own New Jersey model disasters. Gay guys are just slutty assholes." A wise woman once said to me "What's the common denominator in all of your dating life?" I tried to think, "Maybe I was only chasing "hot guys." Or maybe they're all just narcissistic assholes." But she changed the question slightly: "What is the common denominator in all of your dating experiences—in every date you've ever had?"

"Well, yeah, they're all assholes," I insisted.

"But what do all these dates have in common?"

I was stumped. Finally, she gave me the answer: "The thing that all of these experiences have in common is *you*!" She explained that these guys may or may not be similar, but you're the common denominator tying them all together. In other words: if your dating life sucks, it's on you! Here's another way to look at it: "If you spend all of your time chasing assholes, then at what point do you have to get smart and stop chasing jerks?" We tell ourselves it's all their fault, but we never look inward. But whom we choose to pursue is quite revealing about our own character. And if we want a change in our dating life, then we have to start with ourselves, not with blaming everyone else.

Here's another way to look at the situation. You *know* that you've let some good guys slip through your fingers for no good reason. You *know* there is one boyfriend that you treated horribly. I'm not saying you haven't met some monsters. Gay bars and apps are full of them. But you're on those apps getting abused precisely because you let a good guy slip through your fingers. And in that respect, you need to "Blame Yo'self!"

Humans Self-Sabotage

I'm often reminded of that scene from *The Matrix* (the first one, not the shitty sequels), where Agent Smith tells Morpheus (Laurence Fishbourne) that the Matrix program was originally intended to be paradise, where all humans could live out their happiest fantasies. But unfortunately, the human brains rejected a world where everything worked perfectly: millions died in the "happy Matrix," putting the entire system at risk. So the robots created a new system where people could constantly endure the hardships of life. That Matrix worked perfectly—until Keanu Reeves came along. The broader theme about humanity is clear: Humans self-sabotage, and on some level, we are more comfortable with pain than with joy.

I couldn't begin to explain why we are like this, but there is also something inside of us that always wants what we can't have. And if we have a good thing, we'll start focusing on what we can't have or the fantasy of a better thing, and this leads to self-sabotage.

Sometimes it's small. We'll start dating a guy and think, "He's a bit hairy for me," or we'll think, "I don't like his nipples." And we'll use this to start creating emotional distance. Sometimes we'll wait for them to make a minor mistake, so we can justify behaving acting like a bigger asshole. "He kissed a guy in a club, so I'm going to sleep with all of Chicago." As human beings, we are always going to self-sabotage, or at the very least, we will long for what we can't have. The key is to recognize it. I deal with this issue more in depth in the next chapter.

I'm speaking from personal experience here, so I can't judge. I freely admit that I have a VERY strange attraction to people who aren't that into me. It's totally fucked up. But I'm working on it, I promise. No one is perfect, but the more we are present to the messed up stuff we do to ourselves and to others, the easier it is to catch ourselves before we self-sabotage. But we can't do that if we're pretending to be a powerless victim who's at the mercy of evil homosexuals. Here's a hint: *if you like playing the victim, then you're probably a Sleeping Beauty.* You'll start growing and developing only when Prince Charming comes along. But if you haven't trained this emotional muscle, you're going to blame him too.

Don't Get Bitter, Get Better!

Once you blame yo' self, you can change yo' self. Again, you can't change the entire gay scene, but you can change yourself. Write down a list of things you can change about yourself! It doesn't have to be a long list, but actually think. Keep in mind, not all of them have to be deep philosophical revelations. Some can be superficial if you want. The key is to be responsible for yourself. Don't be a victim. Change what you can to make yourself ready and attractive to Prince Charming.

Minor things:

- Can I change my appearance?
    - Nicer clothes
    - New haircut
    - Working out
    - Can I get a new/better profile picture?
- Can I change how I chat?
    - Can I speak in complete sentences?
    - Maybe I refrain from sending cock pics to people.

Deeper things:

- Can I change what types of guys I'm chasing?
    - Can I spend less energy on people who aren't keen on me?
- Can I look for ways I might be sabotaging myself?
- Can I change how I react when guys don't give me the answer I want?
- Can I be more open to guys who aren't my ideal type?
- Can I change how I react to people online?
    - Maybe I need to tell people that I'm looking for a relationship rather than hookups/NSA.
    - Maybe I need to ask people to meet for a drink before sleeping with them.
- Can I change how I reject other people? (Karma... It's real!)
- Can I reflect on what I've done wrong in the past?
    - Take the Douchebag Test and gain new insights
- Can I apologize to people and make amends to others I've hurt? (Again, good karma, and it makes you a better person for Prince Charming.)

There are loads of things you can do immediately to change your dating life. Now some of the items above were more superficial, but that's not inherently wrong. If working out gives you confidence, then do it. It certainly did wonders for me. But also, if buying a new coat or getting a new haircut makes you smile, then by all means, treat yourself. You're responsible for owning your own attractiveness, so work with what you've got. But be sure to do this while you're also working on your personal growth and development in addition to the superficial things. The key is to **get in action!** The mere act of starting to change things in your life that you've identified as needing improvement will boost your confidence. You'll take pride in the fact that you used to be one way, and now you're something different. You caused that, and it will be an achievement. You'll feel less like a victim and less cynical about gay dating. All of this is going to make you more attractive to your Prince Charming and make you a better boyfriend.

Commandment III:
Thou Shalt Not Seek Perfection
(Someone Ugly Loves You!)

One of my friends once told me, "I knew I needed to get off of Grindr when I was looking at a hot guy's photos, and I thought to myself, 'Meh, I don't like his nipples.'" Yeah, that was a good call. With endless choice, some gay guys are becoming pickier than ever before. That's not an inherently bad thing, but we're becoming picky only with regards to physical attraction, and that's going to create problems in forging relationships.

Because Grindr so overwhelms us with choice, after a while, we put our brains on auto-pilot. We stop thinking critically about relationships, even though we know that's where we meet the majority of our potential dates online. We become like dogs chasing cars, constantly searching for the prettiest face or the "biggest zucchini."

Personally, I am a sucker for a pretty face. I always fall hard for a pretty face. And because all we can see are the photos, Grindr and other apps focus us only on the hottest ones online, not the ones who would make the best boyfriend. Grindr makes a potentially harmful proclivity even worse (for me anyway). We obsess over finding someone hotter. We dismiss good, albeit more average looking guys, overlooking their good internal qualities in the hopes of finding someone with all the physical attributes we want. But as we become pickier, we find new excuses to write people off. As with my friend, nipple size can become our sole criterion.

Although that's an extreme example, I think it's becoming a widespread problem. We are, in fact, looking for perfection—or at least what we think is perfection in that moment (or maybe just the hottest guy on the Grindr grid). The result is we become obsessed with looks. If you asked me (and the majority of guys on Grindr) "Are you looking for perfection?" I'd say, "Of course not." And yet I'm always focusing on the guys who are closest to physically perfect or "my specific type."

The result is that this hyper-selectivity on physical appearance cuts off great potential relationships for people who don't meet our insanely high standards. Hell, we probably don't even fit our own insanely high standards. The great paradigm shift between the "old days" of six years ago and the new Grindr age is that now rather than looking for reasons to keep a good guy around, we are focused on looking for reasons to cross him off of our list. **We focus on what quality a guy does NOT have, and we use any minor flaw as justification for crossing him off our list, so we can move on to the next guy. All of his good qualities are ignored; we just know (or hope) that we can find someone better. And with the unlimited choice in a large city, finding someone better is indeed possible, but it's not conducive for finding a great relationship.**

A year ago, I was chatting to a super-hot guy on Tinder. He was a singer from "New Jersey."[3] We had matched on Tinder for the third time, and I was proposing we finally meet for a drink. And after not responding much to our previous matches, he asked me why I was still single. That was an odd thing to ask. I wanted to say, "Because hot guys like you are morons and don't text back!" But I held that one back. When I asked him why he was still single, he said, "Because I'm waiting for everything to be perfect."

I was shocked. "Perfect?" I asked. But he doubled down; he said he didn't want to have any doubts in his mind about whether he should date a particular guy; everything had to be perfect if he was going to commit. Wow. That's incredible. As human beings, we will always have lingering doubts or random fears that pop

---

[3] See :Why I hate guys from "New Jersey" in Commandment VIII.

into our heads. So waiting on a magical feeling to inspire you or the hottest guy you could ever obtain is a recipe for failure.

I knew my muscles had made me picky, but I've never desired perfection. Or so I thought! When I looked closer to myself, I saw that while I didn't call it "perfection," I was always looking for someone "better" than the guy who was presenting himself right in front of me.

The Endless Quest for Something "Better"

Sometimes it's easy to spot when other people are looking for perfection. Few people would say that someone has to be perfect in order to date them. But in a weird way, while I rolled my eyes at the Jersey singer's search for perfection, I realized that I searched for perfection by another name. It's called "waiting for someone better."

For me, now that I have muscles, the super-hot guys are obtainable—at least for one drink or one shag. I can't hold onto them, but I can get a really hot one into bed once every few months. Inevitably, these gorgeous guys are never keen on a relationship with me, but in a weird way it gives me a twisted sense of hope. A hope that a "better guy" will appear in some time, and this awesome better guy will eventually want to date me. Eventually, I find a super-hot guy, and I get my hopes up. Maybe I get him into bed, but then it always ends with me sad about him not being keen on me, so I go out looking for another hot guy.

Many times, I have resolved to be less picky and superficial. I'll lower my right swipe standards on Tinder. I'll start giving "the less attractive" a chance to wow me with their personality with their opening sentence (and keep in mind, I know that there's no way an initial online chat can be substantive). I may even go on a few dates, but the instant a hotter guy appears... Jackpot! I'm already imagining us married. I'm suddenly too busy for the guys that aren't gorgeous, but I will always make time for the super-hot ones!

I've been looking for a hot guy with a brain and a heart for years, and I haven't found him yet. So at what point do I begin to put love over appearance?

Examining my own behavior (and watching my friends), I'm starting to conclude that unconsciously, the desire to always be searching for someone "better" is part of the male condition. I'm starting to suspect it's a smoke screen, albeit an unconscious one. I say that I'm all about relationships, but my actions are showing me that I'm just as superficial and vapid as the gay guys I condemn in other areas of this book! Holding out for someone better is an excuse to keep shagging the hottest guy available and not give anyone else a chance. I may be the only one, but I'd ask my readers to take a moment and reflect: do you unwittingly push away good guys, because you secretly want someone hotter? If so—and even if it's a lesser extent than what I do—we have to consider that maybe the problem isn't Grindr per se; the problem is the man in the mirror!

The problem is "seeking perfection" (or looking for someone "better") and building a loving relationship do NOT MIX! They are completely incompatible. It's no coincidence that out of all of my relationships, the one that treated me the best was NOT the hottest boyfriend I ever had. And the hottest boyfriend I ever had treated me the WORST.

Finding a super-hot guy on Grindr who's got a good personality and a good heart and is interested in dating me is about as likely as scientists' discovering that unicorns do in fact exist. In theory, it seems plausible. Could nature in fact create a horse with a horn? Yes, but it's just not there. Again, perhaps it's unreasonable for me to expect someone to see my unique value based solely on one picture—even if I do have nice pecs—when this guy will always have numerous other dating options.

So when am I going to learn my lesson? But that doesn't mean you can't learn from my mistakes. I could write an entire book about reflections on chasing super-hot guys, but let me give you a brief synopsis on my conclusions on the subject.

Hot Guy Psychology 101

Personality is like a muscle. If you don't use it and develop it, it will atrophy. And once a gay guy discovers he's insanely hot, his personality is no longer needed to get him dates, so he has every incentive to stop using it. And because he has so many options, he doesn't need to treat people nicely to get more dates. He's always got at least 20 people lined up to have a shot with him. So the super-hot guy will never value a non-super-hot guy because he simply has too many choices. And if the super-hot guy never sees value in people who are less attractive, chances are he'll start acting like a dickhead much of the time. And he can get away with it, because gay society won't ever punish him for acting bad.

Ironically, this then sabotages the hot guy's ability to grow and develop as a person, because he's never been confronted with a situation where he is forced to modify his behavior in order to get prospective boyfriends or keep a good one. He's never lost a good thing and thought, "Gee, maybe I need to act better next time in order to find or keep a boyfriend." So, in my opinion, super-hot guys are far less likely to reflect on their behavior and they, consequently, will be far less likely to sympathize or empathize with other gay men. Hence, they are more prone to act terribly with no consideration for how they hurt others.

If he does something horrendous and the aggrieved gay guy tells him off, he can erase or stop such interaction with the push of a button: Block! In the real world, if someone acted like a jerk, he'd have to look you in the eye, at least for five minutes before ignoring you for the rest of your life. But in those minutes, he could see a human being. Not to mention, other people might see him acting like a jerk too. But online, you can be silenced and removed by pressing one button. All your thoughts, feelings, pain, love—everything—can be made to disappear instantly. So no wonder hot guys online are acting like total dicks. The rest of them are the enablers! We are turning them into narcissists with our constant barrage of offers for dates and shags.

The hot guy, more likely than not, isn't going to have a developed personality, and he isn't going to be capable of meeting your emotional needs. So in one sense, maybe it's unfair to ask him to be more than what gay society has asked him to be already. Remember my sister's advice: pretty boys make bad boyfriends.

The Hot Guy Pyramid: Average Guys Who THINK They're Hot

This douchebag mentality that makes super-hot guys bad boyfriends is not just restricted to the top 1% of the population. This mentality is filtering down, and I'd say it's definitely infiltrated the top 50% of gay society—maybe even the vast majority of 60% or 70%. Numerous times, I've dated guys who were cute but not gorgeous, but they certainly thought they were God's gift. I've often found myself wanting to say, "You do realize you're not that hot, right?"

This perplexed me for a while, and although I can't be certain, I do have a theory. I call it the hot guy pyramid. On one level, attractiveness is a completely subject quality. Not every straight man is going to find Scarlett Johansen attractive. But given what modern society tells us is attractive, we can notice a general trend. There are certain people that are more likely to be deemed "hot" than others by mainstream society. There will be a few super gorgeous guys at the very top. And there will be far more average Joe's at the bottom, and there will be plenty of ugly dudes at the very bottom—like a pyramid.

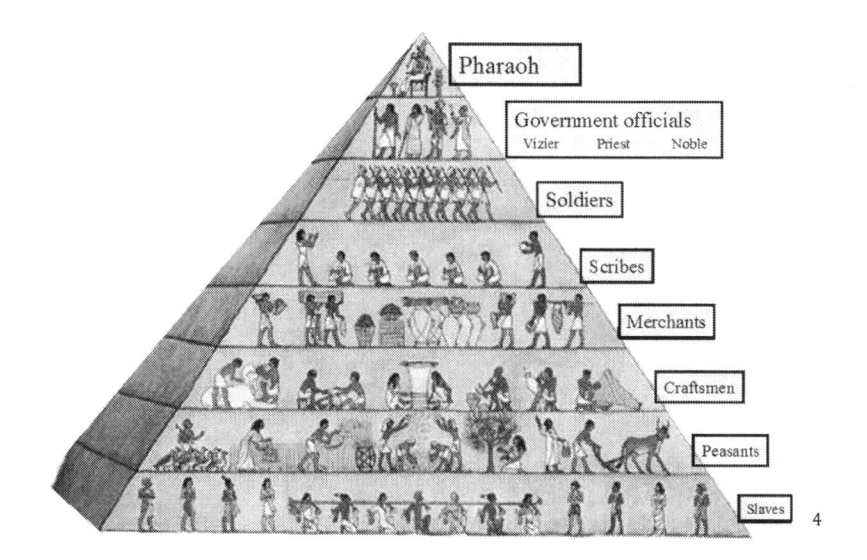

[Pyramid diagram with labels: Pharaoh; Government officials (Vizier, Priest, Noble); Soldiers; Scribes; Merchants; Craftsmen; Peasants; Slaves]

If you're on one of the middle layers of the hotness pyramids, you can experience what it feels like to be a "super-hot guy" on Grindr because you're still "super-hot" compared to the guys at the very bottom. They may not be "your type," and you may not be that hot, but you still get LOADS of dating options. Eventually, all of those dating options will give you perverse incentives to act like a douchebag, just as it does to super-hot guys. In short, average guys are starting to act like super-hot dickheads, because they still have lots of ugly people hitting on them online. So more and more people are developing a bad attitude online. As we gain more options, we become pickier and ruder to those we find less attractive.

Of course, few of us realize what's really happening. We're not enjoying all of the attention we're garnering, because we're constantly looking for perfection or someone better. A few months ago, I was moaning about being single and not finding a boyfriend, but I went through all of my apps, and I thought, "Even if I had no superficial criteria at all, there is no way I could date everyone who wants to date or sleep with me." That was cold comfort when the super-hot Jersey guy didn't text back, but I digress...

---

[4] Image source unknown.

Online dating's emphasis on appearance is making us obsessed with dating people on the "higher rungs" of the pyramid and less likely to date people on the "lower rungs." Ironically, people on the "lower rungs" would marry us in an instant, but we don't care. I know this analogy seems nasty, but I do think it warrants some truth. The analogy is nasty because we're nasty! Because we're so blinded by a pretty face (or whatever quality we desire most), we're ignoring all of the other people who are keen to try to get to know us. So that leads me to the sub-title of this chapter:

Someone Ugly Loves you!

Or perhaps another way to put it would be: someone less conventionally attractive is far more likely to fall in love with you and want a committed relationship. (That's a mouthful—and not in the fun way.) **So gay guys need to be very clear about the fact that we're chasing perfection, rather than looking for love.** But going back to my second commandment of Being Responsible, I'm forced to ask myself, what kind of a moron am I being for always chasing the hottest guys?

Stop chasing perfection and start finding someone who could love you

This is much easier said than done, and I freely admit, I probably fail this commandment the most. But we've all got to, at the very least, open our eyes to what we're really looking for online. Some of you might be telling yourself, "Well, I'm a bit picky when it comes to online dating, but once I meet a guy, I'm really open minded." Well, that might be true, but chances are, you're lying to yourself. Because the desire for "perfection" or someone "better" bleeds out into the real world; it becomes particularly pernicious when it comes to first dates or early dating. We are not only obsessed with what Mr. Right must look like; we've also become equally picky about how Mr. Right must behave on our first dates. If he doesn't look, sound, and act perfect, we strike him off our list and move on to the next.

Gay Dating is Like a Doomed Space Shuttle Crash

Early dates are often like doomed space shuttle launches. They start out with great fanfare; there's much celebration and hope; everyone is excited about the future. And if one person is super keen, the hope is tempered by apprehension and suspense: it's all on the line... But if everything isn't perfect at the beginning... If the slightest little detail is off... BOOM! The date can blow up in spectacular fashion, and it can end in utter disaster and catastrophic failure: with one person vowing never to speak to the other guy again and the other guy being devastated. Again, this is just a by-product of too much choice. Why give someone a second chance if you have ten more guys lining up to take his place?

The by-product is that we instantly reject whatever behavior doesn't look like perfection to us. Said in a different way, we are too wedded to our notions of what Prince Charming is supposed to look like and what he is supposed to do when he first shows up. As a result, we dismiss whatever doesn't fit our notion of acceptable (which is usually unobtainable perfection anyway,) be it in looks or deeds.

The problem is first dates can be awkward. Good people can have a bad day; they can be tired, nervous, unsure, stressed with work, or any number of things. If you're not careful, you can dismiss a genuine guy due to a minor mix-up.

I thought I was open-minded about these types of things, but an awkward first date proved otherwise. Last summer, I went back home to visit my family for a month—which is three-and-a-half weeks too long when you come from a rural, homophobic red state. But in that time I had an experience that made me see how the overwhelming number of choices just sabotages me completely.

So I'm stuck at home, and I decide to go on a date with this guy named Awkward Aubrey. He was super cute, but my date with Aubrey was one of the most awkward in recent memory. We didn't have much in common, other than we were both tired of living in a redneck state. The conversation consisted mainly of discussing how backwards and intolerant the local people were.

But about 40 minutes into the date, two of his friends "coincidentally" showed up at our bar. Now, you don't have to be a relationship expert to see that he asked his friends to show up and rescue him. His friends were both from Latin America (Aubrey is American but speaks fluent Spanish), so to make an awkward situation even worse, the three of them began having a conversation totally in Spanish right in front of me. I don't speak Spanish at all, so I was left sitting there completely lost at my own date. This lasted for at least 20 minutes. I was furious. I felt disrespected and confused. I excused myself and went to the bathroom in order to figure out how I was going to extricate myself from this unpleasant event.

When I returned from the bathroom, his friends were gone, and he suddenly asked me if I wanted to go to another bar. So now I felt really lost, but I put my cards on the table: "What the hell was going on with you and your friends? If you were having a bad time, just come up with a reason to excuse yourself. Why have a conversation in Spanish right in front of me?"

"Well, I asked them to come, but I asked them to show up before I met you," Aubrey said.

"Are you serious?" He asked his friends to show up before he met me, just in case, he was having a terrible time!?! Now, I think he's nuts! Well, at least he wasn't having a terrible time, but I'm still annoyed.

So trying to be a gentleman, I tried to bring the date to a good conclusion. I told him that I'd be up for hanging out again, but I needed to get home. He suddenly changed; now, he was trying to change the conversation to keep me around. He started asking me questions about my academic background and career. It's rare that someone asks me about anything "intellectual," so I was happy to stay and chat about myself (again, all of us gays have a touch of narcissism); he seemed genuinely impressed. Flattery will get you everywhere with me. And out of the blue he kissed me—passionately. Between his kisses and compliments, he kept me out for another four hours, as we were starting to have fun. But at around 1:00 a.m., I asked him if he wanted to come back to my place (Again, I'm not against hookups if it feels organic), but he refused. He said he just *knew* I was going to "use him" for a quick shag and then toss him aside, but he kept trying to kiss me. At this point I was getting sleepy, although I was still feeling slightly frisky but also slightly annoyed. So he protested my advances, except he was still kissing me and complimenting me, but it would all go back to "I'd pump and dump him." (He didn't use that phrase, but I think it's funny.) But after 30 minutes of this game, I was more sleepy than anything else, so I sent him home on his way. Between the Colombians and the hot and cold game, I thought, "There's no way I'm going to date this guy, even as a holiday romance."

In a large city, I can be picky. But the realities of small town life quickly kicked in. It's actually frightening, as in palpably scary, when you scroll through Grindr and you can't find anyone cute who wants to chat with you within 60 miles. Panic sets in: it's like you can't breathe. I had gotten so used to an abundance of dating options, I couldn't fathom not having anyone to date for another three weeks. Again, a few weeks is not the end of the world, but to me, it felt like an eternity. Heaven forbid I focus on my family for three weeks. Of course, they all go to bed by 10. My sister's now married with two kids, and most of my straight friends are married with kids too.

But Aubrey was just so weird, and he wasn't interested in sex anyway. So what's a gay boy to do? I just decided that I'd be friends. Better to have a gay friend than no friends at all. I love my family, but a guy needs a break. So Aubrey and I hung out as friends for a few times; nothing happened.

Then one day, he asked if we could hang out at his place on the other side of town. A fair request, because the gay bars are close to where I stay when I'm in town. But to my shock once at his place, Aubrey made a move on me. I wasn't sure what he meant by this, so I just left. But we talked things over, and he admitted that he's just super cautious about who he sleeps with because he had been hurt before. But he assured me that he liked me the entire time. Once I got past his crazy paranoid "hot and cold" routine, I found that I liked Aubrey a lot. We dated pretty solidly for two weeks until I left my family and went home.

When I started focusing on his good qualities, I saw that he had a lot of them. And they far outweighed the bad ones I had chalked up on the first date. In fact, he was sweet and caring. I found myself reflecting on the plane ride home, "Andrew, if you had been in a big city, you would have never met up with him again. So what does it say about you that you were so quick to cut him off?" I saw clearly how easy it is to write people off when you have Grindr in a city with a large gay scene. I had become so convinced that dating someone had to go in a precise way that I just rejected anything that didn't conform to my pre-conceived notions. And even if he seemed awkward at first, we weren't fundamentally incompatible.

The Desert Island Test

Here's a great way to tell whether you're seeking perfection in how you require your dates to progress. Think about the last few first dates you had recently, and visualize ones where you didn't text back a guy who was keen on you. Take a moment and visualize, what specifically didn't you like, particularly with regards to his behavior. What was "wrong with him"? If he was just way too ugly for you, then that's one thing. But if you didn't click, think about why you didn't click. Do this with a few guys who were keen to date you, and see if a pattern emerges. The obvious common denominator between you and all the guys you've rejected is *you*. So there may be something there, even if you don't realize it.

- Did he seem genuinely interested in learning more about you as a person?
- Was he intelligent?
- Was he more interested to relationships than NSA/hookups?
- Did he make you laugh?
- Do you have common interests?
- Is he keen to see you again?

But if you're nixing guys based solely on superficial reasons, then you might be chasing perfection and not realize it. The key is to start bringing some critical thinking to your dating life and how you analyze whom to date and invest time into.

If you're starting to see silly reasons as to why you never texted back, then ask yourself the following: ***If you were stuck on a desert island with this guy, could you work through whatever issue came up? Would that issue dissolve over time?*** If the answer is yes, then you're probably looking for perfection and don't even know it. If your answer was "If I were on a desert island with this guy, I'd probably kill him and eat him for sustenance," then yes, you made the right choice in not texting him back. But the key is to begin to distinguish how you're looking for perfection and not letting good guys get to you. So maybe give that awkward guy a second chance.

In Aubrey's case, circumstances forced me to work through my issues with this guy and continue to invest time into him. Even though he acted awkwardly at first, I saw that I could be far more compatible with people than a first date might lead me to believe. I don't have a hard and fast rule on whom to date and whom to pass over. But the point is this:

Be open to people and experiences that don't look perfect or ideal at first sight!

Do you have to date an ugly guy to get love? Of course not, although it's more likely to happen... lol. But we've got to understand that your ideal guy emotionally probably isn't going to look like your ideal guy physically. If you want to hold out for a super-hot guy, that's fine. But you may be waiting a long time. If you're starting to think you might be looking for perfection yet you're unaware of it, then read the next chapter where I distinguish what you NEED from what you WANT.

Commandment IV:
Thou Shalt Know Thyself
(Know What You're Committed To!)

The Oracle of Delphi was famous for giving two bits of advice: know thyself and nothing in excess. Well, gays aren't ever going to adopt the second bit, so we better double down on the first. Know thyself!

Not understanding this commandment is probably the main reason you're still single. So perk up. Don't read this chapter with Netflix on in the background, because finding a future husband depends on it! I'm going to suggest something radical here. And if it seems counter-intuitive, stay with me for a while:

If you were totally committed to having a boyfriend, you'd already have one.

What is a Commitment?

Have you ever had that moment in life where you were absolutely committed to doing something, no matter what anyone told you? You put your mind to making this thing happen, despite the odds or difficulties. You tried your hardest; you inevitably hit some bumps in the road, but you kept at it. And remarkably, the universe allowed a few miracles to show up. And either with a bit of luck, or through sheer willpower, you made that thing happen.

Maybe it was something as minor as planning a holiday, or maybe it was embarking on a new career. But when we're rock solidly committed to creating something—rather than just sitting on our butts wishing for some lottery fantasy to come true, we're in the right mindset to make things happen and attract good things in our direction. That's the mentality you must have. Wanting a boyfriend can't be a lottery fantasy; it has to be something you're committed to having for your life.

Another way to look at it is to imagine that one of your parents needed an experimental new treatment, which was wildly expensive. In that instant you'd resolve to do whatever it takes to get your parent that treatment; nothing would stop you, and new possibilities would spring to mind. You'd cut down on small things; you'd campaign; you'd ask people for help; you'd meet with journalists and politicians. That's a commitment!

So when I say, you'd have a boyfriend already if you were genuinely committed to it, what do I mean? I don't mean you spend every waking moment on apps, trying to get dates or shags. Ironically, that becomes counter-productive. I'm saying you don't have the right mindset to make a relationship happen.

Confronting the Myth That You "Can't Find a Man"

If we stopped listening to your whining and only looked at your actions, what would we discover? Do your actions demonstrate commitment to finding a relationship?

Here's a great little test. If I went through your phone, I guarantee that I'd find some phone numbers of decent, cute guys that you just let slip through your fingers. Maybe you weren't paying attention. Maybe you were playing hard to get. Maybe you got distracted with other things. Maybe you didn't think he was hot enough. But if we sat down and analyzed all your text conversations over the past few months, it's likely that at least one of them would hypothetically make you a good boyfriend. Someone who knows himself knows when he's got numerous opportunities and works with what's available. He doesn't whine about not finding the right guy, while passively sitting back, hoping a fairytale prince will appear.[5]

Action Point:
Look For Chats That Grew Cold on Various Apps

I recently got a new iPhone. It can transfer all of your text conversations from one phone to another via the cloud, but that takes up a lot of space. So before I did the transfer, I went through my old phone and started deleting old text chats from the past two years, since my last phone upgrade. I was astonished at the number of conversations that had just gone cold. And keep in mind, these were the ones that I hadn't deleted. (If someone doesn't text me back, I usually delete his number and the chat.) So for me to leave the conversation intact means that I didn't think the person was rude or crazy. They just didn't grab my attention in a major way.

I deleted around 20 different sets of conversations. For some, I didn't even recognize their names or faces or remember them at all. I was shocked. I complain about the lack of good guys pursuing me, yet I found plenty of numbers where I just hadn't followed through. Of course, they didn't chase me either. But there's still something for me to consider regarding my own behavior and outlook. Any one of these guys may have been a great guy or an awesome boyfriend if I had given him a chance or put in a bit more effort. But the truth is that I really wasn't committed to having a boyfriend—well, not to the extent that I tell people I am. I was passive and nonchalant and let the chat grow cold.

Go through your phone right now and look for old chats where the guy was nice but the chat just sat there, neglected. It may be in your texts, WhatsApp, Facebook, Instagram, or even old

---

[5] Again, if you're stuck in a far-away desert or an isolated environment like the North Pole, then yes, you might not be able to find a man. For everyone else, you gotta check your mentality and commitment to finding the right guy.

Grindr, Tinder or dating app conversations. Look at the tens if not hundreds of guys where there was some initial interest, but no one followed through. Maybe he asked you out, but you were busy or never followed up. Maybe he never got back to you, and you weren't keen enough to send him a follow up or reminder text. The point isn't to beat yourself up over not chatting with everyone.

The point is to see how absurd it is for gay guys in the thousands (if not in the millions) to complain about not finding a good man, but no one is ever expending any effort to make it happen. This attitude is so pervasive that, like oxygen, we've stopped noticing it.

Action Point:
Scroll Through Your Contacts

Another way to try this is to look through your contacts folder. Scroll through and see how many numbers of guys you've accumulated over the years. If you're like me, you probably saved the name and the app (i.e. Gary Grindr, Timmy Tinder) where you started chatting. If so, they pop up quickly when you type in Grindr into your contacts.

In my case, I had "James 4 Tinder." If you do this, type in Grindr, Tinder, Hornet into your contacts, and look at the sheer number of names. My phone had 147 guys with the last name "Grindr" and 245 guys with the last name "Tinder." Awkward.[6] Now I'm NOT recommending that you message all those guys, although if it's not too inappropriate, you can always send a text if it wasn't too long ago. The only point here is to get clear about how much choice you have (and you didn't even realize it). So if you're drowning in options, then what's wrong with this picture?

---

[6] Again, these were numbers of people I didn't ever meet, and they include not just people I've chatted to over the previous two years but all of the people I've chatted with during my times of being single since I got an iPhone in 2010.

If you're not laughing, crying, or feeling majorly embarrassed, then you need to take five minutes and try harder. Let the absurdity of the gay community seep in. We've all been incredibly stupid in the mentality we bring to dating. We tell our friends that we really want a boyfriend, but we just treat online dating as an irrelevant pastime, even though it's our primary source of meeting people. We scream and cry that we can't catch a good one as we drown in a sea of options. That's on you. You're doing that. You're responsible for that.

Yes, undoubtedly, some other guys didn't text you back (and in those cases you should delete them and move on), but you didn't text back a lot of guys either! You passed over some good guys. And now you're home alone reading a book on gay dating! As Dr. Phil says, "How is this working for ya?"

The notion that you can't find a good guy is a MYTH! You just have the wrong attitude about dating. "I Can't Find a Nice Guy" is a LIE we tell ourselves. We're drowning in a sea of options, but we just don't realize it.

Personally, I felt a bit shocked by all of the numbers I found. I had to ask myself, "What the hell is wrong with me?" Apps give us so much choice that it's hard not to get distracted. We're like a dog chasing whatever car passes by on the street. It's absurd and funny on one level. But on another level, it's a tragedy. We're doing this to ourselves. It's not just individual self-sabotage, but it's a group neurosis. It's a bit like Republicans denying climate change. The lie has gotten so big that eventually, people just convince themselves that global warming doesn't exist. But in our case, we have brainwashed ourselves to believe in scarcity while drowning in a sea of options. That's "knowing thyself!" Whether subconscious or not, the myth of "I can't find a man" enables you to stay dead—either as a Sleeping Beauty or as a Shagging Zombie. You may cry and scream about wanting a boyfriend, but your actions show that you're really not that bothered.

So now you have two choices (1) accept and embrace that you're not committed and be okay with where you are, and save your friends (and yourself) from having to endure your incessant whining; or (2) change your mentality. Accept that in the past you were dead or not paying attention. Take responsibility and resolve to find an awesome relationship. Make it something you're willing to work towards. You don't necessarily have to expend more time and energy finding a new date, but be aware and present when you're on apps or chatting to guys via text. You'll soon realize that you can have a great relationship if you're committed to having one.

Identifying What You Must Have Vs. What's Icing on the Cake

The problem is that we don't **really** know what we want in our future boyfriend. We think we do because we've all seen Disney movies and think we know how they're supposed to go. But consider that all of these crazy notions from movies, combined with all of the dating options and superficial selection process, have left you unable to choose, intentionally and consciously, what characteristics you need to be happy. You just mindlessly go onto the apps, hoping a fantasy will come true, but you haven't spent any time thinking about what qualities you're committed to having in a boyfriend.

Between Disney's *Frozen* and cock pics at breakfast, we've spent little time thinking about what we are actually *committed* to having in a boyfriend. We haven't analyzed what we really *need* to be happy (our must-have qualities) from what is merely icing on the cake (non-essential qualities that are nice, but you don't need them to be happy in a relationship). We confuse every silly desire that pops into our head as the legitimate voice of reason. We follow those silly thoughts for a while, but like a dog chasing a car, we quickly forget and start chasing something else. But these silly thoughts are making us miserable: we sabotage ourselves with our notions of perfection as we tell ourselves we can't find a nice guy, all the while drowning in options.

Many of you reading the past few pages may be wondering, "Well, come on, we're obviously not compatible with every guy we chat to." True. But once you're **committed** to finding a great relationship, you need to begin asking yourself:

- What do I **NEED** in a relationship to be happy?
- What are the core things that I **must have** for the relationship to work?
- What qualities are nice to have, but I can live without them (aka icing on the cake)?

Another way to look at this is: "if the guy I'm currently dating has all of my must have qualities, what can I honestly learn to live without but still be happy and fulfilled in the relationship?

Now this will inevitably change over time. It may change while you're reading this chapter. But it's okay to spend some time thinking on this, and it's okay to change what you're looking for. But in order to break the cycle, you must start distinguishing what you **must have** from what are random wants or desires that pop into your head. And you must make your dating choices consistent with whatever you decide to write down. You get to choose, and you're free to change your mind at any time. Just bring a new level of intention to your online interactions.

Here's why it's essential to distinguish what you must have from what's icing on the cake: every man you meet will have some flaw. There will always be a silly reason to chuck him out and move on to the next guy. But once you've gotten present to how silly we all act when we're choosing men online, you'll be smarter about in whom to invest your time. And when you're choosing whether to date a guy, you will be assessing him from a mindset of looking for a boyfriend—not just whatever dumb idea pops into your head on how he doesn't look close enough to Chris Hemsworth. This technique helps you to get smarter about whom you associate with. As you distinguish what you need to be happy versus what's icing on the cake, you'll feel more confident in your decisions. Likewise, you'll spot the jerks earlier on, and you can move on faster and waste less energy.

Action Point:
Identify What You Must Have and What You Can Live Without

Grab a pen and paper or type it out on a computer, but create one column with things you **Must Have**, and create another column that lists **Icing** or qualities that are nice, but you can live without them.

Qualities that I *must have* in a relationship

1)
2)
3)

Qualities that are merely icing on the cake (they're great if I have them, but I can live without them if the guy has all the must have qualities):

1)
2)
3)

Now this may either seem super easy or super hard. If it's super easy, maybe you have too many qualities in the *must* column, so many that it may be your unconscious way of staying single. Alternatively, you may have numerous things in the *icing* column that you think are must haves. But that's okay; the key here is to start thinking about these things in that context. If you have a firm grasp of what is merely icing on the cake, you'll stop judging everyone by perfection.

Yes, You Can Be Superficial

Be brutally honest with yourself. Don't be afraid to put superficial qualities in your must have column. There is nothing wrong with desiring a particular quality. There is nothing wrong with saying to yourself, "I need [X] to be happy." It's your life.

Figure out what you must have and go find someone with those qualities. The problem is everyone is pretending not to be superficial, while judging everyone else by unrealistic standards of perfection, and then moaning that they can't find a boyfriend. Know thyself!

Here are my MUST have qualities

1) Intelligence: He must be smart enough that I can have a conversation with him about politics, life, gay culture, and he can keep up and contribute.

2) Handsome: he must be cute enough that I'm proud to call him my boyfriend.

3) Fun: He must be funny and fun to be with.

4) Value Me: He must see my value as a human being. He needs to see that I'm NOT fungible. He needs to see my unique qualities and be like "Oh wow." Not "Meh." (He thinks I'm a catch.)

I learned the hard way to adopt #4. I chased beautiful guy after beautiful guy who just didn't appreciate me. And finally, after one too many incidents of my efforts backfiring, I got tired of it. And to the extent that a guy doesn't meet these four criteria, I now stop all communication and investment of my time and energy. But I **must have** these four things for me to even begin to explore dating someone seriously. Notice that they contain both physical and emotional criteria. Yours should too.

Now here are some things that are icing on the cake for me:

1) He's gorgeous—no surprise there

2) He likes science fiction and 3D movies

3) He can cook

4) He is handy around the house

5) He's into politics

6) He works out

Are you beginning to catch my drift? But these things get a bit trickier when it comes to physical appearance and sexual matters. I have a girlfriend who is very wise and insightful, and when we started talking about relationships, she told me that a man *must* have a "large zucchini" to get with her. She knows she needs that to be happy, and she's fine with that. So if that's on your list, it's okay.

Again, there's nothing wrong with your criteria. Know thyself! Know what lights you up and excites you, both physically and emotionally. Embrace what you want. The key is to keep it balanced and be on the lookout for BOTH internal and external qualities. And if someone doesn't fit your ideal vision for perfection, look at him from the perspective of "Does he meet my core needs for a relationship?" If so, but he isn't perfect on the bonus items, see if he has the good emotional qualities. He probably has some good qualities that you didn't even know you'd like.

Alternatively, if you go on a date with a gorgeous guy, don't just fall for the pretty face, like I do. Ask yourself, "Yes, this guy is hot, but does he have any personality traits that show he can meet my emotional needs?"

If you need a guy who's gorgeous or has a perfect body, then you have to accept the fact that there aren't a lot of gorgeous men out there who are also smart, funny, and kind-hearted. So maybe you'll get the pretty face and that's it. But if that's all you really need to be happy, then go for it.

Alternatively, if you *need* a super-large zucchini, then be prepared to cross off a lot of good guys who don't match that criterion. If you need a particular rare quality, you're narrowing down your dating pool significantly. So you may have to cultivate patience or be willing to tolerate some negative qualities, but that's the level of commitment you need to find a relationship. Know what you must have and what you can live without.

The problem arises when you let one physical quality trump all the emotional ones.

I have a friend named Size-Queen Simon, who is handsome and intelligent and always gets loads of hits. Yet Simon is always single. Part of this is because Simon is a Size Queen. While there's nothing inherently wrong with that, I've watched him repeatedly date guys who were horrible people, who just happened to be hung. He got involved hoping that they would be open for something more meaningful when from the beginning it was obvious that these guys had nothing to offer him emotionally. Simon tends to shag first and look for intimacy afterwards, but given the realities of Grindr, that's not going to work for finding love. Let's be honest. We've all done this in one form or another. We have all fallen for the pretty face or the large zucchini when we knew that they had nothing else to offer, but we kept hoping and praying a miracle would occur. That's a recipe for disaster.

But it may take a few more bad dates or bad experiences to help you realize what you really need and what's just icing on the cake. But just stay thinking and committed.

As we more clearly distinguish what we actually need to be happy, we're more motivated by our commitments rather than by silly random wishes that pop into our heads. We're no longer capriciously crossing people off of our list: we're choosing what we want in life.

Also, this may sound hokey, but I believe that when we're in the right mentality to find a relationship, we attract the right people. Having a mentality of commitment changes our focus and our energy. We're being active; we're empowered; we're in action, working towards a goal. We're sending out the right vibes for future husbands to pick up.

Commitment vs. Compromising

Commitment is different from compromising. If you sell out on what of you must have, you won't be fulfilled, and you won't be able to fulfill your boyfriend. *Compromising* is now a dirty word in the gay world. All your gay friends (at least the single ones) will say, "Don't compromise your standards." But as we've already discussed, you're secretly looking for perfection or at least for someone better. Once you realize what you can live without, you won't feel like you're compromising. You're powerfully choosing what you're committed to having in a relationship, and you're powerfully choosing to let go of things you can live without.

When you're committed to having a great relationship, you'll become the thing you want to attract in others. Will you still meet jerks? Yes. Will people still flake on you? Yes. Will you still get your feelings hurt on occasion? Definitely. But when you're absolutely committed to something, these obstacles aren't as traumatic. First, you've probably gotten much better at screening out assholes, so it's happening less frequently. Second, you don't agonize over losing people when you can see that they didn't have much to offer you anyway. The key is to start judging people on criteria other than your base instincts on Grindr. It's as simple as just asking yourself a few basic questions and following through on your own answers.

Bonus Points: Grade Guys By their Personality

If you're like me and you have a nasty habit of dating pretty boys—or guys with large zucchinis, or guys with a particular characteristic that ends up getting you in trouble, here is a bonus opportunity to moderate those effects. Don't do this for the nice guy who's making an effort—only when you meet those guys and your gut tells you it won't end well.

Next time you go for a drink with a guy because he was super-hot, and you ignored your personality criteria, grade the hot guy by their personality alone. No matter how the date goes, come home and grade him. On an A-B-C-D-F grading scale, assign him a letter for the following criteria:

- Intelligence
- Sense of humor—fun to be around

- Common interests
- Ability to hold a conversation
- Enthusiasm to be there with you

Rate him between an A or an F on each of these. I guarantee he probably flunked most of those. Even if he's super gorgeous, rating him by his personality will at the very least help you take the rejection better should he not text you back. If he does, then you know he might be a keeper, and you might have to expend a bit of extra effort to reel him in. But either way, this exercise will force you to start thinking about what personality characteristics you need to be happy. It forces you to begin balancing your physical attraction against your emotional needs. And you'll be a lot more empowered moving forward.

Commandment V: Thou Shalt Conversate!

Have you ever been in a situation where you chat on and on for ages, but the chat never goes anywhere? Grindr has made sex so easy that we've forgotten how to relate to people on levels other than their appearance. So perhaps it's not surprising that communication skills are on the decline. Without genuine communication you can't show your off your best personality traits. No wonder all we're left with is cock pics at breakfast!

If you choose to chat to someone online, treat it like a mini first date. Don't just give one-word answers. Engage in real conversation. That's how you let the guy know you're interested and worth investing in.

And yes, you might have to message the other guy first or put in a bit more effort than what you're used to. Be flexible and let the conversation flow. But often online, before you've met someone, it's hard to get past the same inane blather. The key to online chatting is figuring out whether this guy is worthy of your time and whether he has any of your must have emotional qualities. But alternatively, if he's ignoring you or just giving you one-word responses, cut it off and move on. But this chapter focuses on situations resembling a two way conversation.

Here are some basic questions you should ask when trying to decide whether you want to continue the chat or meet someone for a drink. You're free to amend these and fit them to you, but they'll give you a good guide, and they'll clear up at least 95% of your doubts.

1)   What Do you Do for Work?

Now you can't judge a book by its cover all the time. But what someone does for a living gives you insights into that person. Most adults spend half their waking hours at their job. So it's a legitimate question to ask. If he's a lawyer or doctor, you know he's smart. If he's an accountant, he's probably smart but an introvert or boring—just teasing; I've met a few fun accountants, but a lot of them were a bit bland.

Sometimes certain jobs are obvious warning signs of trouble ahead. For example, if I chat to a guy who is an investment banker, then I know he's going to work insanely long hours and won't have much time to meet me. Likewise, if he's a professional model, then chances are.... Well, I don't need to finish that sentence.

That's something I'd be like, "Oh cool, tell me more about that." (Hint: By the way, if you do work a shitty job, be super prepared to have your hobbies, passions, interest ready to answer! Yes... Yes... I hear what you're thinking: we shouldn't judge others by their jobs, but we all do it. So take the advice. When you talk about your passions, that comes through even in your texting. The point is to find an area where the two of you can connect and have a stimulating conversation.

And if someone is in a dead-end job they hate, look at how they are handling it: do they have a plan to move one? Are they still approaching it with excellence and commitment, or are they merely putting in their time, doing the bare minimum? You can tell a lot about a person's character in their approach to their job. How men approach their careers can give you insight into how they will behave in a relationship.

2)   What Do you Do in your Spare Time? (Hobbies? Interests? Travel Destinations?)

This one is obviously the most critical because if you're dating someone, you'll be spending a fair amount of free time together.

But this gives someone the opportunity to express themselves and share their passions, even if they have a crappy job.

Pivot To Your Passion!

By the way, I'm not advocating blocking someone just because they may not have a prestigious job. Some people don't have the educational opportunities as others. Some people are doing a shitty job while they are pursuing other hobbies or interests. But this is one factor to give you some insight into the person. If you're doing a bad job while you pursue your dreams, pivot to your passion or other outside interest that really inspires you ASAP. "Well, I work at McDonald's but I'm really passionate about painting."

On the one hand, people often say the same stupid stuff: "I like to hang out with my friends." That's not going to get you a boyfriend. Pick something that is interesting and might elevate the conversation or pick something you think he will relate to. Another way to phrase this question is "So what are you passionate about?" That's a far more engaging question than asking if he drinks beer with his mates on weekends.

2A) Look for Specifics. What's your Favorite Hobby, Vacation Spot, TV Show, etc.?

This is just a follow up to the last question, but getting specific gives the other guy more opportunities to throw out a subject where you two can connect. At the least, it gives him an opportunity to share more about himself—and we all love that, honey!

When the guy says, "I like traveling," you respond, "Have you been anywhere cool recently?"

Or if the guy says, "I like movies," you say, "What's your favorite genre?" Or "Did you see the new Jennifer Lawrence movie?"

These specific follow up questions may not be necessary, but it's just a way to give this guy one last opportunity to impress you and vice versa. I freely admit I'm a couch potato. I love film and TV way too much. But I know that about myself, and I'm okay with that.

Everyone has a secret passion or interest that really lights them up. If you find it out, that's an opportunity to connect with that guy and move the conversation off of Grindr. So for me, I'm a massive sci-fi buff. And I LOVE 90s Star Trek shows. I will date almost anyone if they love *Voyager* or *Deep Space Nine*. So if someone throws that out, instant yes. (I'm such a nerd! Hmmm... Maybe that's why I can't find a man.) But ultimately, you want to find something more about the guys you chat to than mundane questions. If you can find what he's super keen on, you're increasing your chances of getting his number.

3) What are you Looking for on Here?

This is one of the most crucial questions, but the problem is that people LIE all the time on this one. But for me, if people overtly state that they are looking for a relationship, then they get bonus points because it means that they're not complete commitment-phobes. And if the guy openly declares that he's only after random sex, then I know I should leave him alone. The key is not to assume that everyone on Grindr is a slut or to assume that everyone on Tinder is a saint.

Gays Have Made Relationship a Dirty Word!

The problem is people lie about what they're looking for all the time. Often, slutty guys want sex from guys who aren't so slutty just to avoid STD's. Sometimes, other guys are afraid to say that they're looking for a relationship because they don't want to appear desperate or needy. In the age of Grindr, hot guys have so many offers for sex that they literally don't need to settle down. So as they get comfortable with only looking for NSA, the rest of us become scared to articulate that we're looking for more. Or we've been hurt so often that we've just given up.

I struggle with this one too because, let's face it, a lot of hot guys are sluts. On the one hand, you want the hot guy to be interested in you. But on the other hand, you don't want to look like you're desperate and might come across as a stalker. And let's be honest, we all have a level of hotness that if someone offers us NSA, we're not going to say no—no matter what our internal integrity tells us. So I'm not shaming you for hooking up with that super-hot guy.

The danger and the resulting upset come from wanting more than what the other guy is open to giving. Several times a year, I'll shag a super-gorgeous guy, but it NEVER ends in a relationship. I keep hoping that my razor sharp wit and charming personality will change his slutty desires, but no such luck; I need to accept what they're offering—a one night stand that may or may not be good—and move on. But overall, sluttiness is so endemic to the gay community, that I fear that articulating an interest in a relationship scares people. We've made *relationship* a dirty word.

Tip: in these types of situations where you want to be cautious just say, "I'm looking for **dates**."

While I'm hoping to transform the broader consciousness of the gay community, I want you the reader to get laid and have numerous potential boyfriends knocking at your door. So we have to accept the world we're in while simultaneously seeking to change it. So my advice is: say you're looking for DATES. The term *dates* can be more casual or more serious, depending on the other person.

If you want to aim for something more serious say the following: "Yeah, I'm looking for dates mainly, but I'm not really into NSA." This lets the other guy know you're not easy, and it will screen out a lot of the perverts and sex addicts. And it will also screen out the people trying to catfish you, because they won't want to meet for a drink in a public environment where you can walk away. You don't look desperate for a husband and signal that you're not easy. But you take the risk of disappointing the super-hot slut and having him stop chatting. You get to make that choice. Just be clear that he's not going to change for you.

Alternatively, you can make *dates* a bit sluttier by saying, "Yeah, I usually like to meet for a drink, but we all have needs, right?" Or... "I'm looking mainly for dates but open to occasional fun." This lets the guy know that you're still up for getting down and dirty, but again, if he's more relationship oriented, then you may look like a slut.

Some other variations of this include:

- "Ultimately, I'd like to find something more substantial, but the chemistry has got to be right."
- "I'm looking for something more long term, but happy to do mates and dates till then."
- "I'm ultimately looking for a boyfriend, but I'm really picky, yet I'm open to whatever."

These are some ways where you can hint that you want more than NSA but not look like someone who's using Oprah's "Secret," praying for a boyfriend every day.

3A) "No Agenda" Is the Worst Response Ever

I HATE people who say, "I don't have an agenda," or "I'm not looking for anything in particular." First, you're fucking lying! We ALL have an agenda. Grindr is one giant clash of agendas! We all want something. It's either to get laid, find a boyfriend, or get an ego boost. All Grindr activity leads to one of those three destinations. So let's be honest with ourselves.

If someone gives me the "no agenda" line, I try to push back gently. "Everyone's looking for something on here ;P" That's when I might add what I'm looking for. But if they stick to the "no agenda" line after you've told them you're looking for dates, then they're either sluts in disguise or completely wasting your time. Either way, they probably won't make a good boyfriend. Just look at this in the entire context of the conversation and see how you feel.

4) What Kind of Qualities do you Look for in a Guy? (Use Rarely)

Use this question only if you're looking for a long-term relationship and he says he's also looking for a long-term relationship. But this is a way to find common ground. How people respond is EXTREMELY telling about what they are really looking for. If the guy lists superficial qualities (aka big cock, blond hair, muscles), then you probably know he's not a deep or thoughtful person. If the guy lists emotional qualities (kindness, big heart, thoughtful, caring), then you know you've got someone who is more relationship oriented.

5) What's your Longest Relationship? (Use Carefully *BEFORE* you Meet)

Use this VERY carefully. Don't bring this up in the wrong context or early on in your initial chats. It needs to flow out from a nice conversation that's moving in the right direction. But it gives you immense insights.

I was chatting with a guy in his late 30s—tall, Australian, very handsome. We met for coffee. And we were talking about dating in a big city, so I asked, "So what's your longest relationship?" He came out with, "I've never had a boyfriend before."

What...

The...

FUCK!

I was very polite. And I didn't blow up. But I wanted to scream, "WHY DIDN'T YOU TELL ME YOUR ASS WAS CRAZY!" RED ALERT. SIRENS.

All of this was blaring in the back of my head. If you're 21 and never had a boyfriend, that's fine. But if you're knocking on

FORTY and never had a relationship, then something is definitely wrong. This guy was stunning, but it ended up being a complete waste of time. What's worse is he demanded we meet on the other side of town, so I traveled for nearly an hour to meet him, and I had to travel an hour home. My afternoon was completely wasted because I didn't ask this guy one simple question before we met up.

Yes, you can't judge a book by its cover. And if he had pursued me and shown some real interest, I would have explored it for a while. But he didn't, and I wasn't surprised. Another great reason to read this book while you're young is that people will forgive certain flaws in your 20s that become deal breakers when you're getting close to 40. At that age, far more people are husband hunting, so deal with your craziness NOW. Don't be like the hot Australian.

6) What are you Into Sexually (Sexual Position)? (Use Only After 10pm)

This is another question to use VERY CAREFULLY. If you're looking for a relationship, you'll look like a slut if you ask it too quickly without context. Yet it's really important to ask. I have gone on dates and could feel myself falling for guys who were not sexually compatible with me.

I met another guy from New Jersey (are you noticing a pattern) last year, and he was perfect. Beautiful, but not so beautiful that I felt ugly by comparison. He was toned and had a good job. I suspect that there were other issues at play, but he cut things off because we weren't sexually compatible, but I certainly tried. I ended up with a broken heart, a sore ass and no boyfriend. Grrr.... So yeah, make sure this comes up BEFORE you meet him for a date.

Again, it's all about context. My rule of thumb is that I only ask this question late at night after 10pm. If the guy tells you he's had a drink or two that evening, then it's fine to ask then. If you ask that question in the morning, when people are headed into work, you look like a sex addict who doesn't have anything else to do in life. Ideally, it will flow organically from the conversation. But if it doesn't, you throw it out carefully. I sometimes phrase it as: "I'm not trying to put the cart before the horse, but I am a bit curious, what's your sexual preference?" Or another option might be "I try not to judge people's sexual position based off their photos, so I always like to ask, just to see if we're compatible."

The Gay Danger Zone: Half-Assed Responses

Personally, I hate it when I'm chatting to a guy and he's not really responding promptly, or when he does, the responses are short or closed-ended, and he doesn't ask any questions back. That's where things get confusing. Is the guy busy with other stuff? Is he just distracted? I often turn the apps on while watching TV. And it's hard to have a deep conversation when you're watching Chelsea Handler. But in general, if the guy isn't asking you any questions back, then he's not really that keen on you, and he's just wasting your time. Depending on the context, he might be telling you that he's not interested. If he's not interested in hearing about your day in a text, he for damn sure doesn't want to hear about your day in person.

Another thing to watch out for is people who just parrot back the question you just asked them without taking it any further. I call this the "and you" response, and it's annoying as HELL!

> Hey. How's it going?
> 11:53 PM

> Good. You?
> 11:54 PM

> I'm good thx. Busy day earlier. 😊

> So...

> You up to much?
> 11:55 PM

> Not really. You?
> 11:55 PM

> Like I said, it was a bit hectic, but things are slowing down now.

> Any big weekend plans?
> 11:55 PM

> Seeing friends. You?
> 11:56 PM

> Going to a friend's leaving dinner. Fancy Italian place.

> So what's your favorite food?
> 11:57 PM

> Chinese food. You?
> 11:57 PM

> Italian, Thai, Chinese, Indian... I eat everything!
>
> So what else are you doing this weekend?
>
> 11:58 PM

> Gym maybe. You?
>
> 11:58 PM

> Gonna' catch up on some TV maybe.
>
> What's your favorite TV show?
>
> 11:58 PM

> Friends... You?
>
> 11:59 PM

Today

> Game of Thrones, House of Cards are my favorites.
>
> Also, I like Orange is the new black...
>
> So...
>
> Delivered 12:00 AM

So, as you can see from the photos above, one person is making an effort to move the conversation along and find a topic of common interest, but the other person is just giving one or two-word responses and isn't making any effort to connect. The second person is only expending the bare minimum amount of effort to keep the chat going, and that's almost impossible to read—other than to demonstrate a clear lack of interest or a lack of emotional intelligence. But that's really unfair to the other person, who's making a sincere effort.

Commandment V

Now, sometimes people are busy in the moment, and they're distracted. Sometimes, it's hard to find common ground so you're just flailing around a bit. But if they never initiate a chat by sending a message first, and they only respond with "[X] and you?" there is a 90% chance that you're chatting to an utter moron, or they're not interested in you, and you should cut your losses and leave him alone. But this is always context dependent. You have to examine the entire conversation and decide for yourself.

And of course, make sure you're not the one giving those half-assed "and you" responses! That's a commandment violation right there! If you're not interested, don't chat. If you are interested, make a bit of effort. You can't expect a different result from Grindr if you never make an effort to get to know someone on a non-superficial level!

Take it to the Next Level

If the conversation is floundering, and he's giving you just enough conversation to keep you from thinking that he's totally disinterested, then take the conversation to the next level. Either ask him out on a date or ask for his phone number. "Hey, you seem cool and interesting, are you up for meeting for a drink some time?"

Asking for his phone number is safer, but there is still a huge risk that the conversation will go flat again. When you ask someone out on a date, they are suddenly forced to view you as a potential date, not just an ego boost. You may not like the result, but he will put you out of your misery. That's not to say the guy won't flake out, but it's better than a "no" or being ignored. Alternatively, if you've hit a stride in the chat, and you've had a good exchange, ask him out. Strike while the iron is hot. You may not have his attention for long, so make the move while you can.

I have a friend named Charismatic Keith. Keith is the best pickup artist I have ever met. He's not ugly, but he certainly isn't gorgeous. But he's the type of guy who can charm owls down from trees. He gave me a bit of advice for online dating: Always ask them out early, like within the first ten minutes of chatting (assuming the conversation goes that long). If they say no or merely hesitate, Keith immediately blocks them. Yes, he cuts a lot of cute guys off, but he's left with people that are very keen on him. Keith is not that picky about whom he dates, and he definitely prefers quantity over quality.

I've tried to adapt this strategy—maybe not within the first fifteen minutes, but I always do it sooner rather than later. People definitely reveal their true level of interest once you ask them for a date.

This commandment ended up being longer than I had anticipated. But in chatting to someone in cyber-space, you can't read their body language or hear the tone of their voice, so you have to be smarter in how you communicate if you want a positive result. The key always is to approach conversations with an openness to learn about the other person and see if that person can has any of your emotional qualities. But this requires that you engage in some real conversation and not just respond with one-word answers. Simply parroting "And you?" is not enough. Inevitably, there will be a lot of hot guys who are just airheads. But better to know that sooner rather than later. Likewise, stay open to the possibility of letting another guy show you how great he is, even if he isn't your perfect type. You might be pleasantly surprised. But all of this leads up to one inescapable truth I have encountered over the past few years of online dating:

If he's not keen to return a text, then he's never going to be keen to be your boyfriend!

I know that's an over-simplification, but I've found it to be 100% reliable. Yes, you might get one or two shags out of a flakey guy, but a lot of disappointment and upset usually follow later because ultimately you're looking for more. People sometimes profess to be busy or bad with texting, but they overcome these flaws if they're keen enough. If a guy's not giving you energy and enthusiasm in your online chats, then you must learn to walk away.

Commandment VI:
Thou Shalt Not Be a Time Waster!

Part of surviving Grindr and online dating is learning when to cut it off!

Just kidding! I mean cut off the conversation, not their cocks. I am not Lorena Bobbitt![7]

Nearly all of my gay drama has stemmed from the fact that there is a mismatch in desire: one person is a definite "yes and the other person is a weak "maybe, leaning towards no." I freely admit I have failed at this one many times. It's hard to cut things off when they're gorgeous and they are responding to you, but doing so in a half-assed way. It feels like torture. I feel like I'm in a

---

[7] For you non-American readers, Lorena Bobbitt was a woman who chopped off her husband's penis with a knife while he slept. She was later found not guilty by reason of insanity. In fairness, the husband allegedly was an abusive prick.
https://en.wikipedia.org/wiki/John_and_Lorena_Bobbitt.

Saw film and have to saw my own foot off when I have to let a guy go.

It can even be tough on the other way around: you're chatting to a guy, he's not your type, but you don't want to be mean or hurtful—and maybe he's liked all your pics on Instagram; he's interested in your hobbies. I get it. It's hard to tell someone who's keen to go away (albeit politely), but you HAVE to do it!

Cut it Off!

When we chat to people online, some guys we see are a definite YES; others are a definite NO, but the MAYBE category seems to be the biggest and most dangerous area to be in. I've been on both sides of this equation, and it's definitely hard to navigate. Apps are making us more superficial and offering us an obscene amount of choices. And after a few bad experiences with pretty guys, I have made many a resolution to be to be less superficial. I then start chatting with people that maybe aren't my ideal type because I want to give people a chance. The problem comes in when you're a "Maybe… If no one else hotter comes around," and he's a "Yes, what chapel do you want to get married in?" So if you're on the other side of the equation where you're the "Meh" and he's the "Definite Yes," you need to find a way to put the guy out of his misery and not lead him on for months on end.

This seems super obvious, and you're probably thinking, "I'm not wasting anyone's time," but we've all done it. We don't think of it so overtly, but any time we're unsure about whether we want to meet a guy and we just keep chatting and chatting and chatting, we're wasting that guy's time—incidentally, also our own. We just want to keep him around in case Mr. Perfect never shows up. But as we discussed before, he's not going to show up. And if he does, you'll shoot him down because you didn't like the size of his nipples.

At this stage, you've got tools for distinguishing whether someone is going to meet your criteria for a date. Be honest with yourself and stop wasting other people's time. If you don't want to enjoy his company (or test his sexual prowess), let him go so he can find someone who will love his ugly ass just the way he is.

Having been on both sides of this coin, I get that sometimes we're unsure. And a lot of people have had really negative experiences with dating. Some people have met real stalkers. Others have had people steal their private naked photos and post them online. Obviously, you have to protect yourself. But you can still be smart about figuring out what you're looking for and whether this guy has anything to offer you. But you have to think actively and intentionally rather than engaging in useless prattle for months on end.

If after all of this reflection, you're still on the fence, then you're probably a No. But when you continue to chat with him, he's thinking you're leaning towards Yes. In situations like this, it's better for you to cut the conversation off so he can move on. Don't be a douche about it! But you may need just to block him online or stop responding to any of his texts.

Know When to Sashay Away

Part of not wasting your time is learning when to "sashay away" rather than acting like a desperate stalker.

(I couldn't afford a photograph of RuPaul, so I'm using the great Vinegar Strokes again as my cheap stand in. I can't risk Mama Ru trying to sue me.) But part of online dating is knowing when to cut your losses and move on. Stop messing with the guys that are just wasting your time or keeping you around like a dick in a glass case: "in case of emergency, break open!"

Let's definitely take some additional advice from a tall, wise African-American man who's made millions by dressing in drag. No, I'm not talking about RuPaul, but I have the nagging suspicion this guy is still "family." I'm talking about Tyler Perry who plays the sassy old black woman named Madea. This video (or a version of it) has gone viral. And I've seen straight, old white men posting it to their Facebook pages as great advice to their kids on relationships. So it's definitely worth a watch.

https://vimeo.com/86149821.

https://www.youtube.com/watch?v=WJ-aWRVm9uQ.

(The vimeo is better quality than the YouTube)

In short, Madea tells you that it's okay to be sad when people disappoint you, but move on with your life. Let people go: if you put forth a good effort to create a relationship with them and they weren't interested, let them go. You'll forget them eventually, and you'll reflect "What the Hell was I thinking? I must have been lonely as hell?"

Madea also made a powerful distinction about people: some will be with you for a life time; others will only be with you for a season. The heartache comes when you can't figure out which is which. Your life is like a tree: most people are like leaves. They blow and fall away with gusty weather. Other people are like tree branches, they seem sturdy, but if you try to stand on them (depend on them), they break, and you fall down. You'll be lucky to find two or three people in life who will be like real roots to you. They're not worried about being seen, but they're always there to support you. I encourage you to watch the video. The message is powerful and applicable to all. But for gay guys in the world of online dating, the message from Madea is **Let them go!**

Get The Hint!

Everyone hates time wasters, but no one likes a stalker either. If the guy hasn't responded after two messages, GET THE HINT. Move on. Stop wasting your time and energy on him. We've all encountered weirdoes who keep messaging us the same "Hey" five, six, or seven times, even though we didn't respond. Sometimes they switch it up to "Hey handsome." Like that's going to work! And then, as a Hail Mary, they sometimes just send a cock pic. Obviously, if any of you out there do that to guys, STOP IT! The guy's not interested. Take the hint.

But that one was obvious. Most people don't do that. There is a far more dangerous gray area that is easy to fall into. It's a minefield, and it will suck you dry and drive you crazy if you're not careful. Getting the hint is harder if he's responding but giving you just the "and you?" routine I discussed before. Remember my tip to "Ask him out." If you've done this and things still aren't going anywhere, or he keeps giving you excuses or flakey reasons, GET THE HINT. Stop wasting your time. Part of being happy in the new age of Grindr is getting smart about walking away from "bad investments" and finding people who are good investments with respect to your time and energy.

To Block or Not To Block? That is the Question!

So if you've tried everything, it's still not going anywhere, and you're still chatting on the app, you may want to just block him and move on. Some people are fine to let the conversation go cold. They do nothing but hope and pray that one day, the hot guy will "break open the emergency glass" and ask them to come over at 4:00 a.m. But that's not me. If I'm chatting on an app, and he doesn't seem keen, I block and move on. If we've chatted via text, then I may just delete the chat or delete his number. Usually, I'll never hear from them again. But sometimes, I will. Again, the gay drama comes from a mismatch in levels of interest. The sooner that you recognize that your level of interest is way out of whack and you're not getting anywhere close to the same level of energy, the sooner you can let them go.

The Pretzel Clause

Sometimes playing hard to get is attractive, and I know that I always end up putting more energy into someone who seems slightly less interested in me than I am in him—in part because I think I'm subconsciously attracted to the chase. But part of surviving Grindr is learning when to walk away. But I have one exception to this rule: I call it the *pretzel clause*. If I am about to block someone or delete his number, I ask myself, "Is this guy SO HOT, SO OUT OF MY LEAGUE, SO AMAZING, that his hotness merits me turning myself into a pretzel to keep his attention?" Ultimately, that's a subjective determination. But usually, once I ask myself that question and I take a good look at his photos, I say, "No way." So I block and move on.

Occasionally, I do invoke the pretzel clause, keep their number, and hold off on blocking. But when I say I turn myself into a pretzel, I'm talking one or two extra online messages or texts, or one final request for a date. Don't send that bitch flowers! He won't appreciate them. TRUST ME.

Expend a *minimal* amount of effort just to stay on his radar and let him know you're interested. I call that the pretzel clause because I feel embarrassed and somewhat humiliated chasing a hot guy that I know doesn't have my career goals or intellect. But a few extra chats isn't a big deal either way. It's not like any of your friends will know how desperate you were to get this guy.

I only invoke the pretzel clause two or three times a year. Any more than that, then you're asking for trouble. I've never gotten a boyfriend from invoking the pretzel clause, but I have gotten a few good shags.

Commandment VII:
Thou Shalt Not Be Flakey
(Flakey Men Are the Scum of the Earth!)

I make no bones about it; I think **Flakey Men are the Sum of the Earth!** Well, not literally. But I find flakiness to be a far worse problem than any other issue with gay men in the new era of Grindr and online dating apps, even worse than rampant promiscuity (and that's a big ass problem). But being a slut is just a biological reaction in one form or another. But flakiness, the inability to commit to a date or give people advanced warning that you cannot attend a date, is a serious character flaw. No one in the gay community seems to be addressing this, and it drives me absolutely bonkers!

This chapter has no humor or self-deprecating remarks because it only makes me furious. A man who flakes on you has violated most of the Grindr commandments in one go.

- Flaking on you last-minute is a *douchebag* thing to do
- He's demonstrated that he's *not taking responsibility* for how his actions disappointed you
- He has *not communicated with you effectively*
- He's demonstrated *he's not committed to a relationship* (or open to the possibility)
- And he probably doesn't *know himself* enough to realize how hurtful his flakey behavior is
- *He's wasted your time* and energy (after leading you on)

- His *actions have spoken louder than his words* (see the next chapter)

Flakiness is the antithesis of everything I'm writing to promote, so no wonder it pisses me off so much. Even if it seems trivial to you, **you must honor your promises and take them seriously if you want to find a meaningful relationship**; otherwise, frankly, you're not ready for a relationship. All you're going to do is hurt another genuine person.

I know I've said that everything else I've written can adapted, rejected, or modified, but not this. If there is an absolute truth, this is it. Remember when I said that acting like a jerk has an impact on you, even if you don't realize it. The negative behavior eventually seeps into other areas of your life. Flakiness is far worse. If you don't honor your promises on the little things, such as meeting for a date, you will cop out when you're confronted with a real temptation in a relationship. It may seem counter-intuitive, and many might argue, "Well, I'd flake on the little things but not on big things." But let me explain why not honoring your promises on the small things makes it impossible for anyone to be truly emotionally intimate with you.

Distinguish Flakiness From a Genuine Emergency

So I hear you saying, "Well, what about genuine emergencies?" Of course! My God yes. There are a million reasons why you would legitimately need to cancel a date on short notice, and some of them might even stop you from communicating in a timely manner. But most of these reasons involve a loved one being in the hospital or at death's door. In these cases, Go! Get to the hospital. Don't worry about texting. Go be with your family! Sometimes, your work schedule might change at the last minute, or your boss might drop a project on your desk at 4:59pm. Occasionally, you can be absent-minded and just double-book yourself. These things happen all the time. They aren't that big of a deal, and they can be sorted out.

But in the vast majority of cases, if you need to cancel or reschedule, you can do so in advance, but many guys simply don't. Giving someone advance notice is NOT being flakey because the other guy can make alternative arrangements. **So if something comes up, text him ASAP!**

Even if you think you might have to cancel or change the plans, let the person know ASAP! Better to let him know with three or four hours of notice that there's a chance you may need to cancel than to risk dropping the bomb on him while he's waiting for you at the bar.

But 99% of the time when gay guys flake at the last minute, it is not a genuine emergency. They just couldn't be bothered to make an effort. Here's how to distinguish quickly a genuine emergency from an otherwise minor issue: *Can two reasonably smart people, if thinking together in unison, solve this issue that's arisen?* If the answer is yes, then he's just a flake. If the answer is no, then he's got more urgent issue.

How a man handles committing to a first or second date is very revealing as to how he will treat you for the remainder of your relationship—even if it's a short interaction. If the man gives you advance notice, stays in touch with you after the canceled date, and makes an effort to make it up to you, then you've got yourself a keeper. If he's immature when it comes to treating your time and your feelings with respect, then you should let him go. Otherwise, you risk constantly being infuriated.

So this chapter is dedicated to the men who cancel on you five minutes before your planned date. You're waiting for him at the bar, but he's still at home finishing putting gel in his hair, and he's thinking, "Well, I'm already late. Should I bother? Maybe I should just cancel…."

That type of flakiness and lack of respect makes me so angry I can barely analyze and explain it. Flakiness is like Lex Luthor to my Superman. Flakiness smiles at you, tells you all the right things, and then spends all its time trying to destroy everything you try to create. It's insidious like that. Perhaps, it's more like a virus than a super-villain. But it's serious because online dating apps are the new ground zero for the flakiness virus. And it's spreading.

If a guy tells me online that he's only looking for fun, then at least I know what I'm going to get. And I know that if I try to ask more of him than one or two shags, it's not going to end well. (Sometimes, two sluts can find happiness from a one-off that evolves into more, but that's rare.) But at least the slut on Grindr is being honest with me. There's integrity to what he's pursuing, even if he's emotionally stunted or not ready for a relationship. He's honoring his promise to you (he promises nothing after one shag) even if he didn't give you everything you wanted.

Flakey people are a hundred times worse because they will promise you more, chat to you for weeks or months, but they have no intention of living up to anything they've promised. Or they mean it in the moment, and then at the last minute they just decide you're not important enough, so they bump you. In my opinion the latter situation is far more dangerous, but in either case, the result is the same: the flakey man leaves the normal gay man twisting in the wind. The flakey man has treated the genuine guy with utter disrespect and disregarded his time and his feelings. Here's the sad but honest truth:

You can NOT build any type of relationship with a flakey man!

Nothing! Nada! Zilch! Zero. It's like trying to build a house on quicksand: one person is trying to construct something great, and the other person isn't bothered about whether it all slips away into nothing. If you try, it's going to be a lonely, frustrating endeavor. You'll be doing all the work, and the other guy simply won't care to lift a finger.

Flakiness is a Cover for Lack of Interest

First, let's deal with the flakey man who is using flakiness to avoid the fact that he didn't want to date you to begin with. This situation sucks. But what can you do? This type of flakey man never fancied you that much. If something comes up for him and he doesn't let you know (hoping you won't ask him where he is), or he tells you only at the last minute, then you know you have the worst kind of flake. He's not that into you, but he doesn't want to feel bad about what he's done, so he's hoping and praying that you'll forget about him. That way he can avoid feeling bad about himself—and worse, he can avoid the risk of acknowledging how hurtful his behavior is and seeing your pain.

But you were never going to win with him anyway. A relationship with such person will always be impossible. In a sense, he did you a favor. You didn't have to waste any money buying his flakey ass a drink. And because he was disinterested, chatting to him on a date would be a terrible experience anyway. He'd probably be checking his Grindr every time you stepped away to use the rest room. Even though you're fuming, because you're now stuck at home on a Friday night with nothing to do, you're still better off. But it sucks because he led you on, got your hopes up, and dashed them without thinking twice.

So if his first response is to hide or ignore the issue, then that's how you know you've got someone who is riddled with the flakey virus. After reading this chapter, if he again hurts your feelings, that is entirely on you! You Were Warned!

Flakiness is a Cover for Weakness and Narcissism

This is a controversial statement, but follow me on this one and see where I'm going. The far more dangerous type of flakiness—and the one that's deadly to gay relationships—is the flakiness that is a smoke-screen for the gay man's internal narcissism and overall weakness of character. And it creates a lot of problems because it is far more difficult to sniff out in initial chats via texts. The flakey man will tell you one thing but can't deliver on it. And since you're just getting to know the person, you can only judge him by what he's telling you at the beginning. So even with all of the lessons you've learned so far, you have no idea if you've met Mr. Right or Mr. Flakey until it's too late.

Here's a non-rhetorical question: *What is really going on with a guy who says something in the moment and then later flakes out?* Another way to think of this is: *What's going on in the mind of the flakey man? What's he hiding?*

I know we're not psychics. But just as an exercise, think about it for a moment. This man is partially attracted to you, even very attracted to you. But the flakey man just can't seem to make the first date happen. Or often, you have a great first date, you continue to chat, but the second date just never materializes. What's going on with the flakey guy in that scenario? He likes you. In theory, he wants to date you, but it just doesn't happen. What's up with that?

Pause to think and ponder. Here's the Jeopardy link again if you need the music:

https://www.youtube.com/watch?v=vXGhvoekY44.]

So here's my theory; brace yourself!

Flakey Men are Like Sleeping Beauties on Steroids!

A flakey gay man is often a man who gets easily stopped by the little things in life. When life gives him a minor speed bump, he gives up and turns around or takes a left-turn. He'll probably then console himself with excuses. "I'll try harder next time." "Maybe if the speed bump isn't there." Or "I'll find another path someday—but not today." But again, the result is the same. The flakey gay man will never cross the speed bump because he can't be bothered. But he doesn't realize he can't be bothered. He deludes himself with excuses for not traversing the speed bump in order to feel like he hasn't done anything wrong. He tells himself that life has just given him a big problem, and he doesn't have the energy or wherewithal to deal with it. His little excuses matter more to him than whatever time or energy you've put into organizing the date. In short, he's not willing to cross the speed bump for you. Now no one thinks like this intentionally or consciously. Usually this happens very quickly and last minute. But it's a very weak way to go through life.

Like Sleeping Beauties, flakey men must have everything perfect, easy, and convenient in order to grace you with their presence. Relationships are not easy, and they are often inconvenient. So a flakey man will not have the requisite commitment to make a relationship work. He never thinks to ask himself, "If I can't overcome a small problem to attend a first or second date, how can I commit to a relationship?" It will never occur to the flakey man to put any energy or time into overcoming an obstacle to meet his promises. If it's not super easy, he's out.

Consequently, a flakey gay man can't grow because he lacks insight into himself and how his actions affect other people. As a result he doesn't see his flakiness as a problem. To him, the world is big, he's small, and that speed bump in the road is Mount Everest—just too steep for him to climb, or so he tells himself. But to him, it's a reasonable way to respond to a problem that he doesn't want to deal with in the moment, particularly if he's been tempted with another offer to go out that evening.

The problem is relationships are *always* hard work. They will always have obstacles to overcome. But many of us—both flakey and resolute—often have the idea that a relationship will be like a Disney fairytale. But even when Prince Charming presents himself, and the "Flakey Beauties" acknowledge that their prince has indeed arrived, they will refuse to leave their comfortable bed of excuses until all the stars are aligned. "Wait. There's a dragon outside? And a forest of thorns? Wait, you mean that *I* might have to fight the evil witch? Yeah… Maybe another time…." Back to sleep they go.

Gays often tell themselves, "Once everything is perfect, then I will start working on a relationship." But if a particular moment requires some hard work or inconvenience to achieve, Flakey Beauty ain't getting out of that bed. Even if she knows she's found a good catch. Flakey Beauty doesn't realize it, but she's bailing at the slightest inconvenience.

Now don't get me wrong. Everything is relative in terms of problems we confront in life. And on one level, I can hear you saying, "Who are you to judge?" Well, I'm the guy that has dealt with flakey people for many, many years, and this is just my opinion. You're free to disagree. But keep with me, and you'll see where I'm going.

A lot of men reading this article think they're upstanding gay men, but the flakey virus is ravaging them like an antibiotic-resistant gonorrhea at a chem sex party!

It's fine to choose the easiest way possible when it only pertains to you. One reason Grindr works great for a hookup app is that it makes sex very convenient. Convenience isn't inherently bad. But life is full of inconveniences. And we're developing more and more gay men who can never be bothered to inconvenience themselves, but who spend their time wondering why they're always single. If they do date someone, it's usually someone where the external environment makes things very easy—like a work colleague or someone nearby. And if the boyfriend finds a new job on the other side of town, the inconvenience is more than the Flakey Beauty can handle, and the relationship fizzles out. But throughout all of this time, the Flakey Beauty will never realize that it's his unwillingness to inconvenience himself that is causing all his problems. To the flakey gay man, his reasons are good enough. And they'll happily go back to their slumber until another Prince Charming appears, and all of the surrounding circumstances are easy. At the end of the day, flakiness is the manifestation of a lack of commitment to pursue a relationship in the midst of difficulty. Flakey Beauties get distracted, can't be bothered, or simply don't care.

Here's how you know that Flakey Beauties aren't capable of real growth or real relationship commitment: they turn into dragons themselves if you try to explain how their flakiness hurts your feelings or ruins your evening. These bitches *hate* to be told how their flakey behavior hurts genuine guys. When Flakey Beauties flake out on you, their image of Prince Charming is someone who patiently waits and takes whatever little crumbs of energy they feel like doling out from time to time. If you don't say anything other than the following, Flakey Beauty will view Prince Charming as a dangerous threat to his limited selfish worldview:

- "Yes, you canceled on me at short notice but it's okay my darling Flakey Beauty."
- "I'll be fine. Even though I had champagne waiting on ice for us, that's okay. Don't worry about me."
- "When everything is perfectly convenient for you, I'll be here waiting...."

If you don't completely absolve them, they turn into nasty bitches. Anything else will be met with hostility, because if you try to express your hurt feelings, you'd be confronting them with an insurmountable mountain: taking responsibility for their flakiness and expending energy to make amends, which threatens their entire worldview. To continue to date you after they've flaked out, Flakey Beauties would have to change their outlook and realize that the speed bump was a molehill, not a mountain. And once they accept that, they'd inevitably be forced to consider a number of unpleasant realities.

Maybe being stuck in the tower is actually their fault?

Maybe they've hurt numerous guys with their flakiness?

Would they have to make amends to others?

Would traversing this speed bump become a regular thing? That prospect is terrifying.

All of these things threaten the worldview (and slumber) of Flakey Beauties, so despite their claims to the contrary, it's easier for them to wait for someone who is charming *and* convenient. If you dare try to nudge Flakey Beauty from her myopic standpoint, you will have a massive bitch fit on your hands. Flakey Beauty will soon despise you if you don't immediately acquiesce and pretend everything is okay. She will attack you for being a jerk for confronting her and not instantly forgiving her for ruining your evening.

Flakey Beauties are just Douchebags in Disguise!

Our Grindr and dating app culture is making it easier and easier for Sleeping Beauties and Flakey Beauties to stay stuck. We can treat others like they're easily replaceable because they are. Why reflect on your bad behavior and make amends if you can just find someone else. So we end up with a community where everyone is dead and lifeless and refusing to make any effort. This leaves everyone unhappy. But the numerous choices stop us from growing or waking up. This flakiness, resulting from the broader lack of self-awareness and lack of empathy for others, is **the** most insidious part of Grindr. People tell me that they're up for something more, and they want to break the cynical cycle, but in reality, they just can't be bothered to expend any effort.

I'm not being hyperbolic when I say flakiness may be the worst problem affecting gay men. Yes, apps make us more superficial. We can scream till we're blue in the face about how gay culture puts way too much emphasis on appearance. But people can't help whom they find attractive; those issues are very complicated. Yes, there are a lot of messed up things going on in the media, which set social norms for good looks, but that cake is baked for most of us. We can work on the future of media and culture, but for now, people fancy what they fancy.

But flakiness is stopping gay men from having great relationships NOW! Everything is there—just one person can't get their ass in gear. Or they are pretending and saying all the right things and not living up to their promises. And in that instance, you can't build anything. So in terms of finding and building loving relationships, flakiness is far more dangerous than promiscuity, in my humble opinion.

The Narcissism Test

I've made some harsh conclusions about flakey people, and I remain confident in my assertions. And that's because I believe flakiness is often a smoke screen for narcissism. When the Flakey Beauty is confronted with a minor speed bump, turning around is more important to her in that moment than anything *you* might want. It's the most disrespectful way to show that your time, feelings, and hopes are far down on her priorities. Flakey Beauty will not grow or be pushed to do anything outside her immediate comfort level. She frankly doesn't care if you're hurt or disappointed because she comes first. And if you get hurt, you better keep it to yourself because to say otherwise might expose her as just another douchebag who can't be bothered (and that contradicts her self-image).

The next time a guy flakes out on you with short notice, do **not** tell him "everything is okay." Tell him the truth. Now, you don't have to get crazy. Don't threaten to cut that bitch. Don't curse. Don't lose your cool. But you can be dignified and yet let Flakey Beauty know that you're not okay with his behavior. You can say something like:

- "Well, I spent a lot of time planning this date. That hurts my feelings a bit."

- "With such short notice, I can't really make alternative plans for my evening. That kind of puts me in an awkward position, no?"

- "If you needed to cancel, I understand, I'm just not clear on why you're telling me now at the last minute."

How a man responds to this line of questioning will immediately reveal whether he's a lion or a mouse, so pay very careful attention. Flakey Beauty is like medusa and you're holding up the mirror. He will lose his shit the instant you start pressing him on this. If he comes back with anything like "I said sorry," Or "Why are you trying to make me feel bad?" or "Why are you making a big deal out of this?" then you know in an instant that he's a narcissist who is incapable of inconveniencing himself for you. He will *never* make your needs a priority, and he will *never* put your wishes above his. Flakey Beauty may be hot, but she can't wake up from her own narcissistic fantasies and pitiful excuses.

Again, as I said, don't go mental or ape shit. Say in a calm, collected, concise way that his behavior left you in a tough spot, and that's not okay with you. And if his immediate reaction is **not** one of compassion and empathy, but rather one that's all about him, then that's a hint and a half that he really doesn't give a damn about you. Maybe you planned something nice. Maybe you were really into him. Maybe you had been looking forward to seeing this guy all week. But he doesn't feel the same way. So when a gay man says "Why are you making a big deal out of this" (assuming you haven't turned into a sniveling idiot or a raging monster), what he's really saying is "You are not a big deal to me." He is demonstrating with his actions that he wasn't that excited about a date with you. He wasn't that keen to spend time with you. And he certainly wasn't going to inconvenience himself in the slightest.

By the way, I am NOT saying the flakey guy is a bad person. He is just simply too caught up in his own world to make someone an equal partner. That sucks because he probably had potential. Maybe he'd make a good friend, but he is NOT your future husband.

Tip: No First Dates on Friday or Saturday Nights

Because it's often so hard to tell who's going to flake out on you with no notice, I adopted a new rule that has helped me at least avoid losing a good evening: *never meet a guy for the first time on a Friday or Saturday evening*. Rather, I keep new dates to Monday, Tuesday, or Wednesday evenings. If you have to meet at the weekend, Sunday in theory works, but it's highly likely that either you or him will be hungover. Saturday afternoon could work too. Just don't give a new guy the chance to screw up an evening that might be better spent with friends, family, or a guy who's not flakey.

This may surprise you after reading my manifesto, but I am extremely gracious when someone communicates with me in advance that his plans need to change, so long as he hasn't done it at the last minute or he's responsible about it if he cancels on short notice. I have a lot of compassion for people I date. I want to be there for them through ups and downs. But whether they confront changing plans head on or whether they hide out and hope that I won't notice their flakiness reveals a lot about a person's character. In a sense, flakiness is a deception. The guy you've been chatting to or dating professes to be open to one thing, but in reality, his actions demonstrate the opposite, and you're the one who's left disappointed and upset.

Flakiness is one of those ways that men blind-side you like a Mack Truck. In a world of online dating, where you can't see his facial expressions or his body language, you have no idea of knowing whether he means what he says online. Most of the time, he's flaking because he was never that interested to begin with. But other men use their flakiness to hide some unpleasant truths about themselves. But all of this can be avoided most of the time if you just text him in advance or promptly and you remain keen to stay in touch and reschedule.

Honoring your word and your agreements is key if you ever want to have a deep relationship where you're connected by anything more than convenience. Don't make promises you don't intend to keep. Don't lead people on. Don't use people just so you can feel like you have dating options. Even if you disagree with some ideas in this particular chapter, spend some time reflecting on flakiness nonetheless. Not keeping your word and not being genuine with your intentions have an impact on you—whether you see it or not.

If the signal you send to the universe is that you'll break your agreements when it becomes inconvenient and you don't care about hurting other people, why should anyone commit to you? So for God's sake, **don't be flakey!**

Commandment VIII:
Thou Shalt Judge Actions, Not Words
(I Hate Guys From "New Jersey"!)

First of all, I have to confess that I've never been on a date with a guy from New Jersey. At least, I think I haven't. So why the controversial headline?

Imagine your worst date! I mean the one where you ended up leaving feeling humiliated, defeated, furious, and you wasted a lot of time (and possibly money). Now imagine the second worst date you've had where you felt all those things. Now imagine the third worst date. What if all of these terrible guys came from the exact same location? You'd be a little suspicious, right? I'm not trying to pre-judge an entire group of people, but it's caused me to question a few things. And because I don't want to come across as prejudiced, I'm renaming the location to protect the guilty. So I apologize in advance to New Jersey guys. I'm sure you're lovely.

But all the "New Jersey" boys I have met seem to have an unusual combination of being both very handsome and yet horribly vile in their behavior. (Actually, even some of the less attractive ones are even quite slimy.) I'm not sure why this combination is so intertwined in them. If you recall, my primary upset was with the New Jersey model who made fun of me on Twitter after I sent him flowers. But there have been several other incidents with the Jersey boys that followed. It had gotten to the point where if I messaged a cute guy and he told me he was from "New Jersey," I would politely end the chat and then block him when he was offline.

I can accept the fact that one group of gay guys is shadier than the average. Different regions have different cultural norms, but for the life of me, I just can't figure out why. Why do they act this way? They seem very keen at first; they would lead me on for a while, but then turn horribly cold and mean. And this puzzle drove me nuts. I'm someone who prides himself on reading people rather quickly. The fact that I'm writing a freaking book on gay dating means that I've got an opinion on everything. Usually, my opinions are the result of careful reflection and analysis. Yet the "New Jersey" boy question drove me insane. Maybe because these Jersey boys are hotter than average, they're more prone to act like douchebags. Or maybe "New Jersey" has a lot of religious hangovers and the gay guys act out as a response to their frequent rejection. Perhaps, I'm letting coincidence get the better of me, but there's just no one theory or pattern to make all of the dots connect.

So I finally asked a friend of mine from "New Jersey" about why I constantly was having upsets with these guys. His simple explanation floored me. "[Jersey] guys want to be seen to be being nice, even if they're not interested. So they'll play along because they don't want to be seen as mean." Of course, this explanation didn't explain the Jersey model who was just an asshole. But it did explain several incidents with other Jersey boys. There was an obvious mismatch in interest levels. And rather than doing the usual stuff to let me know they weren't interested, they were going along with things because I was so keen. This inevitably led to a car crash, not to mention, I'm still a bit suspicious of Jersey guys (hey, once bitten twice shy). But this realization hit home a very powerful lesson you've got to keep in your mind in the age of Grindr and all the endless choices that online dating brings.

Judge a Gay Guy by His Actions, NOT by His Words

That doesn't apply only to "Jersey guys." In theory, I should have learned this lesson years ago when I was in a long-term relationship with my then pathologically lying ex. My ex would tell me over and over again about how much he loved me, how special I was, and how he saw a future where we'd be married with kids. A lot of these kind words came after I had caught him cheating on me. That created a lot of distrust and suspicion, but my ex always knew the perfect thing to say to get back into my good graces. I'll never forget that we had gone out drinking one night. He was clearly drunk, and I thought I'd press him for details: *in vino veritas* (that's Latin for "in wine there's truth"). In his intoxicated state, he assured me that the other guy meant nothing to him. He acknowledged he made a mistake, but he assured me that I was his soul mate. So that night after he fell asleep, I went through his phone (yes, that violated his privacy, but I had caught him before), and I found that he had booked a vacation to travel hundreds of miles to see one of the many guys he cheated on me with at a time when he knew I'd be out of town visiting my family. He also had been having sexual relationships with two other guys, and later I found evidence of at least two more. But every time, he'd plead with me how much he loved me. At the time, I was so hurt, vulnerable, and in love with him that I had a hard time learning this lesson. In fact, I didn't learn it at all. I thought, "He was just a complete scum bag," but the lesson is clear to me now more than ever. A guy's actions always speak louder than his words.

It's true that since the age of Grindr, people don't play mind games any more—they just don't care. But that doesn't mean you can't get your feelings hurt. A lot of men (not just gay men) will lie to you to keep you around until they're done with you. That's just human nature. They want to keep you around, and if they decide to settle for you, then they want you there. But if you're not careful, you can tolerate this behavior well into weeks or months of dating.

So we always have to ask, "What are this guy's actions telling me?" Because they are always telling us something! Do a guy's actions demonstrate interest? Or are they demonstrating that they don't care. This situation becomes particularly tricky if they know how to say the right things. If they're hot, and you're already planning the wedding, it's easy to ignore the warning signs until it's too late. You may be on the verge of doing something big to show them that you care about them, and while you're thinking that your actions will sway them your way, you may be in for a rude awakening.

Usually, most people aren't trying to hurt you. It's human nature to want more dating options as opposed to less. And like Jersey boys, they don't want to be seen as jerks, so they tell little lies to try to get out of awkward situations to make things seem less hurtful. So you've always got to be mindful of observing a gay guy's actions and distinguish them from his words. And the following tip applies: if his actions are telling you "no," then you may have to jump back a few chapters and "Cut it off!"

Commandment IX: Thou Shalt Remain Joyful!

God, grant me the serenity to accept the things I cannot change, courage to change the things I can, and wisdom to know the difference.

This is used by people at AA meetings, but I think it's totally applicable to online dating in the age of Grindr. The simple truth that I have tried to accept is:

The Majority of Gay Men Will Never Appreciate Me!

This is not a criticism of gay guys. It's just a simple fact. The majority of guys you chat to online or meet in real life aren't going to be your soul mate. We all want different things out of partners, and most of the time, gay guys don't even know what they themselves really want out of a relationship. Apps make us superficial, and human beings self-sabotage anyway. So inevitably we all will have some chaos, upset, and disappointment in dating. Part of maturing as a gay man is accepting:

If you want to find a relationship, you will inevitably be disappointed and hurt.

You can't escape that. You have to accept it but remain open to taking risks when it comes to your heart. Yes, it's frustrating, but that's part of being alive. Only dead people can't be hurt. And if the spiral of cynicism worked, you wouldn't be reading this book now. Guarding your heart will be ultimately self-defeating, but I think you probably realize that by now.

Think of Dating as Looking for a Good-Fit— Don't Take it Personally

Being hurt sucks. Processing grief is part of the human experience. But you should at least try not to take rejection personally. And a lot of people are just lost and confused and can't appreciate a good thing when it presents itself. Or they come from an environment that's made them too superficial to appreciate a great thing that falls outside their standards of attractiveness (and I put myself in that category too). In today's society, people are a lot more complicated and individualistic. Finding a guy with all of your must-have qualities is going to take longer than you think.

One of my dearest friends is dating a professional ballet dancer named Ballet Bob. Bob is really good at what he does. I've been to a few of his shows. Ballet isn't just a job to Bob. It's his life; it's his passion. It brings him joy. It's a natural self-expression, and that's great. Not to mention, all the ballet dancers have super-hot bodies and nice butts. I've asked Bob a few times to introduce me to some of his colleagues. I'm still waiting, Bob! But I realized that if a hot ballet dancer needed me to appreciate how much he loved ballet, he would be shit out of luck. I hate stuff like that. I'm smart, but I'm not at all sophisticated when it comes to high culture like museums and the ballet. Like most gays, I like a good musical on occasion, but even that's rare. While I could appreciate a ballet dancer's physique, I don't know if I could appreciate his soul in the way that would make him truly happy. That doesn't mean I'm a bad person, and it doesn't mean that the ballet dancers are bad people: it's just all about finding a good fit. And that's how you have to look at it.

Dating is all about finding someone with whom you can connect on multiple levels. That's not easy. You have your own quirks, interests, hobbies, and passions. You're probably funny and witty, or you might be quiet and sensitive. But you're unique, and you have value outside of what other gay men think. Because we have more dating options, we're going to meet more men who inevitably don't fit with us. But don't let the morass and craziness of Grindr rob the world of the gift that you are.

Don't Let Rejection Rob You of Your Joy!

This commandment is probably the hardest of all to accept. It's very "Zen," and I freely admit that I haven't mastered this one. I'm getting better at it, but I've still got a long way to go. It's not easy being open to a relationship (and by extension making yourself vulnerable) and yet being okay with the fact that people will see these amazing qualities in you and opt to pass you by (or worse, do something mean to you). That shit hurts like Hell!

But if you're looking for something more substantial than a one night stand, and you want real love, you have to master the ability to be yourself: be the open, loving, funny, quirky, real you and yet not be devastated when the guy you send flowers to recoils in horror. Yes, it hurts. Yes, it sucks. Yes, that guy is an asshole. No, you didn't deserve that. But the mastery of this concept is all in how you bounce back.

Yes, you deserve time to grieve or process the pain if need be. But just make sure you bounce back at 100%, confident in yourself and confident that an awesome relationship is possible. That's what I mean by "your joy," but perhaps I should use the term optimism or belief in what's possible.

And when I talk about possibilities of loving relationships or being the real you despite rejection, I'm not talking about a Pollyanna-type of existence where you force yourself to be positive about every shitty thing in the world. You don't have to drink cult-like Kool-Aid and keep telling yourself "Everything is awesome." Far from it. Life is full of assholes—gay and straight. And people are going to hurt you. But it's more about a quiet, powerful inner resolve, a determination, rather than forcing yourself to think positively.

When we've been hurt after trying hard to make a relationship happen, it's always easy to say, "Meh, I'm not making an effort next time." Or "I'll just hold back from showing him the real me." So either consciously or unconsciously, you start to suppress the real you, and you let your doubts kill your belief in what's possible. You hide your feelings and emotions. You blame yourself and feel stupid for making yourself vulnerable. You vow NEVER to get hurt like that again, and so you start closing yourself off. You force good guys away. You stop making an effort. You kill off the personality traits that you love the most in the hopes that others will then find you more attractive. And before you know it, you're emotionally dead. You're just another Mindless Shagging Zombie roaming the world aimlessly on Grindr, falling deeper down the spiral of slutty cynicism.

So the key is don't let another gay guy's reaction kill off your own happiness and belief in what might be possible for yourself and your relationships. If you start killing off the real you—the happy you, the imperfect but exuberant you, the quirky you, then you're only hurting yourself. The world does NOT need any more brain-dead shagging zombies. The world needs real gay guys who are sensitive, kind and not afraid to show it. The world needs guys who are brave enough to risk things for love, but not turn into bitter shells when it doesn't work out.

The true test of enlightenment in the new world of Grindr is someone who can move from bad date to bad date to bad date but never lose their inner joy or belief in loving relationships. That's a real man!

If you can be the *real* you, and be totally okay with the fact that most gay guys aren't going to be able to love and appreciate the real you, but you're still warm, friendly, and quirky to every new guy that you meet, then you need to take my place and start writing a book. Like NOW! And I can't wait to read it! But in doing that, you'll be more receptive to someone who does love the real you. When he knows you're crazy but loves you anyway, then you've got a keeper! But if you're bitter, you'll push him away before he realizes what a catch you are.

Get Smarter About Taking Risks

That being said, you can be smarter about when to take risks. You may recall that I once sent flowers to Architect Arnold, and Arnold was so moved that he started looking for a job in my city. Although we didn't end up together, Arnold is one of the sweetest people I have ever met, and I'm glad I got the chance to date him, albeit temporarily. You may also recall that I sent flowers to a New Jersey model who made fun of me on Twitter.

Upon starting the book, I didn't think there was a connection between these two events. It was a total crapshoot. In one instance, I got lucky, and in another, it backfired. I just thought I had to suck up the rejection and not become closed off to taking risks. But after writing this book, it became clearer: the Jersey model was not open to anything romantic from me, but Arnold was. And this was obvious from the way they both treated me via text. The Jersey model had already stopped texting. He only gave me his "excuse" after I followed up a few more times. My flowers were just a stunt to get him to change his mind. I took a chance when all the evidence shouted that he was in no way interested in me at all. But Arnold, although living in a different city, was constantly texting and calling me before I sent the flowers. He was giving me good communication vibes, and it was obvious he was open to something special, as he kept chatting with me despite being far away. It seems obvious now, but I didn't realize it at the time. In fairness, I admit that three years had passed between the New Jersey model and Arnold. But here's my tip:

Only use a grand-gesture when the guy's actions indicate to you that he's open for more! Never use a grand gesture to try to redeem a crappy first date. It won't work. It will backfire spectacularly.

Grand gestures are, well, grand. They're a big deal. And if you create one, they instantly signal that you're keen enough to want a committed relationship. If he's not on the same level (or anywhere close) in terms of wanting to take your relationship to the next level, your gesture won't make you look like Prince

Charming arriving at Sleeping Beauty's castle on a noble steed. It will be seen as a stalker-like way to keep the uninterested guy's attention.

It also puts pressure on the other person to reciprocate. Since you've done something awesome for him, he feels pressured to do something grand in return if he wants to keep dating you. And let's be honest; most guys on Grindr will just run and hide rather than make that kind of an effort.

Small Gestures Probably Work Better in Earlier Rounds:

Small gestures can work well also. In fact, it's better to stick to these when you're in the early stages of dating in order to avoid a massive backfire.

- Offering to cook for him
- Making a picnic in the park
- Taking him to a comedy night
- Treating him to a movie

But context is always key. Make sure he's already giving you time and attention, signaling he's at least open to more. I'm not religious, but Jesus was right when He said, "Cast not your pearls before swine." And Grindr has a lot of pigs. Most guys you chat to online won't deserve any gesture at all—big or small. So get smarter about choosing the right guys to pursue.

Distinguish Changing Yourself Vs. Keeping the Real You

As I said in the Second Commandment, you should be responsible for who you're attracting and letting into your life. You're responsible for the types of guys you pursue online. But you can also work to change certain aspects of yourself. You can be more mindful when approaching others. You can change your outfit or join a gym. You can even get some Botox injections. Doing things that make you feel more confident is NOT the same thing as giving in to hopelessness and bitterness. It's human nature to try to avoid getting hurt in the future, and it's human nature to want to make ourselves as attractive as possible. At some level, you have to accept that most gay guys aren't going to be able to love the real you, but you keep being the same funny, quirky, camp, silly you—all without losing any enthusiasm or joy!

"If you can't love yourself, how in the Hell are you gonna love somebody else? Can I get an Amen?"

Wise words from Mama RuPaul. (Again, I couldn't afford a RuPaul photo, so I'm using Vinegar). Those words take on a different meaning in the context of this commandment. It seems obvious in one sense: of course you love yourself. But you have to love yourself enough to protect your heart so you don't get defeated when someone doesn't return your affections. You have to love yourself enough to keep being the real you. You have to love yourself enough not to let these negative experiences kill your belief in finding love. We can't let hurt and rejection turn us into mindless shagging zombies. Don't let some asshole from "New Jersey" rob the next guy of getting to know the real you. Someone out there will love you just the way you are.

Commandment X: Thou Shalt Not Heed The Noise!

So, you've successfully navigated Grindr. You've gone on a few dates with a guy who doesn't flake. You two get along. Then what? Are you really ready to delete all of the apps? Do you stop meeting other guys? This book isn't a relationship book. There are loads of those out there, but this book is designed to help you navigate Grindr, empower yourself, and consciously choose whether you want a relationship or whether you're happy being single. There's no right or wrong answer to that. Yet often gay guys sabotage a relationship in its infancy for no good reason.

As Grindr makes it easier to hook up or find new dating prospects, the apps give guys fewer incentives to commit: why commit when there is always someone new available? Why commit when someone better might be just around the corner? So commitment isn't just a dirty word; it's becoming a foreign concept that fewer people are exploring or experiencing, and that's a problem. What's the gay community going to be like in 10 or 15 years when the majority of guys on the scene have never engaged in any sort of serious or committed relationship? What will it say about us if few people know how to create an emotional bond that can truly last for years (not to mention, the rest of our lives)? I'm not saying every relationship has to be a traditional monogamous relationship, but a true emotional bond is going to require more commitment than what we're experiencing on Grindr. And let's face it, a lot of gay guys are afraid of commitment! Men in general are scared of commitment, but Grindr has exacerbated this problem for gays a hundred fold. And this fear can sabotage a good thing.

"I'm afraid of people who aren't afraid of commitment." We may not think about it that overtly, but that's what your actions may demonstrate contrary to what you believe about yourself.

I'm afraid of people who aren't afraid of commitment

Suddenly, the idea of cutting off all the potential dates can be frightening, particularly if you haven't done it before. We may have been praying for Prince Charming to arrive, but once we're confronted with the notion that living happily ever after means deleting Grindr, we will squeal, squirm, and freak out. All humans, whether gay or straight, male or female, can suffer from a fear of commitment. But Grindr makes it worse.

Whenever I go into a committed monogamous relationship and delete Grindr, for the first few days or weeks, I find myself a bit sad and upset. Yes, my new boyfriend is a nice guy, but I find that I actually grieve for my Grindr app in a small way. I've become so accustomed to having it and turning it on when I travel to different places that it's hard to kill the impulse.

And I miss the ego boost of numerous men throwing themselves at me every day: getting to flirt with cute guys or even stare at amazingly hot torsos. I even miss the cock pics with my cheerios.... Just kidding; it's not that bad. But you get the point. As

I discussed before, the ego boost from online apps stimulates dopamine levels in our brain, so in a sense, the Grindr flattery becomes addictive like a drug. We so rely on our daily injections that when we don't get it, we go into withdrawal. Even if we're not "clinically addicted" to Grindr, we can become accustomed to the stimulus, and so it's natural to miss it a little bit if we're entering in to a new relationship. I call this Grindr Grief, and it is going to come up, but it will pass in a week or two.

Problems arise when we interpret the reaction of "Grindr Grief" as something inherently wrong with our relationship or something wrong with our new boyfriend. There is nothing wrong with him, and there is nothing wrong with our new relationship. The problem is **WE** ourselves. We're just reacting to the lack of stimulus that we've grown accustomed to. But these addictive thoughts will tempt us to do something that will sabotage the relationship if we're not careful. Don't give in to those negative thoughts. You're on the verge of having a potentially amazing relationship. Don't sabotage it because you're experiencing a bit of Grindr grief. I promise, it will pass!

It's Natural to Have Some Commitment Jitters

Take a situation outside of dating, such as your career. Have you ever resolved to get a new job or get a promotion for work? You saw what you wanted and you become determined to get it, no matter what. What happens then? Like an avalanche, every reason why you can't achieve the success, the impossible odds, the fear of failure and humiliation, or even the time commitment seems too great, or the new job is too far away. All of this comes racing into your head. And just like that, you conclude, "Meh... Why bother." It's the exact same dynamic in relationships.

The instant we commit ourselves to something that might require real hard work and sacrifice, our mind comes up with all of the reasons and excuses of why it won't work out. These commitment jitters are just fear of the unknown or fear of commitment. We fear pushing ourselves in new directions. We fear sacrifice and compromise. And even though we may tell our friends that we want a boyfriend, often we may be too comfortable in our ways to embrace change even if it costs us awesome relationships in the long term.

But these commitment jitters only want one thing: to keep you stuck in the status quo. Yes, being single sucks, but you've gotten comfortable with it (although you may not realize how comfortable you are). You may secretly like the attention, the thrill of meeting new people, or the freedom to do whatever you want. Part of you may want more, but why take the risk of getting hurt? We human beings are creatures of habit and comfort, even when the status quo isn't ideal.

As humans, natural selection has taught us to survive, not how to live fully engaged in the moment. Right now, you're surviving Grindr, not using it as a tool to bring you happiness. Cultivating a new relationship in the era of Grindr will not be comfortable and easy, and part of you on some level is going to resist this change.

We all are uncomfortable with change, even if we know it will be for the better for us in the long run. So we can never eliminate those random fearful thoughts. But if we're committed to having awesome relationships, then we won't let this brain noise stop us from exploring all the great things that are possible in relationships.

Commitment Jitters Disguise Themselves as Other People's Flaws

Few people realize what's going on. They don't realize that their fear of commitment it trying to take control; they'll just suddenly feel overwhelmed by a sea of doubts that pop into their minds. For me, the instant I get into a committed relationship mwith a guy, my mind goes into overdrive, and I begin to see every little flaw in him with precise detail. And those flaws become magnified, and they gnaw at me in a way that didn't bother me when I had the option to date other people. These flaws haunt me like ghosts in an old mansion. I hear a little voice whispering, "If only he did this... If only he did this one thing, then I could really love him." Or worse, I often find myself thinking, "If only he were a little bit hotter, I could really fall for him." Or "If only he had six pack abs, then I could really love him." These haunting thoughts can last for months, long after the initial Grindr Grief has passed. But if you're not careful, you'll start believing those haunting thoughts, and they will sabotage your new relationship.

My very first boyfriend—let's call him Norm—Norm Hull because he was just a *normal*, average guy. (But it will take scholars decades to figure that one out.) Norm was a decent guy; he was fun but a bit of a drifter. He was nice to me, but he had this giant mole on his chest. It irked the fuck out of me for months. I'd stare at it all the time whenever we had our clothes off. It just bothered the hell out of me. I despised it. I often fantasized about getting a carving knife out of the kitchen and just cutting it off myself as he slept. Obviously, over time it didn't bother me as much. And after we broke up, and I realized I'd never be with him again, I missed him—and that ugly mole of his. At the time, I would have welcomed that mole back with open arms. I would have given it a big kiss if I could have (Ewww... maybe not). But you get the point. When you're confronted with commitment, you suddenly start looking for petty reasons to distance yourself.

Maybe for you, it's not an ugly mole. Maybe it's the size of his ears, his receding hair-line, his annoying laugh, but something like that *will* pop up at the beginning of your relationship. The key, however, is to get that it's not him, it's **you!** You're unconsciously sabotaging your relationship. STOP IT!

As human beings we're hardwired to want what we can't have. When we're single, we long for someone who will be with us through thick and thin, someone to cuddle us when we're lonely and make us laugh when we're sad. And when we're in a committed relationship, we long for the days when we could do whatever we want, go clubbing and kiss boys, or get cock pics in the morning with our cheerios, etc. We're always going to have those thoughts, and no person can stop those thoughts from occurring, no matter how "perfect" he is. It's just human nature. You're going to have random thoughts and feelings in a relationship, and a lot of them are just stupid and nonsensical.

So the key is to realize that not every thought that pops into your head is divinely inspired or a great revelation for mankind. You're not Plato or Nietzsche! You're just a gay dude who wants to see a cock!

Humans are prone to think stupid things. It's going to happen whether you want it to or not. So be mindful of it. Think of it as an old air conditioner (or maybe a dodgy boiler if you live in a cold country). It's always grumbling and whirling in the background. It's on; it's part of your home. It's going to make noise, and you can't turn it off. It's always going to be there. The key is to just accept that it's just noise, and the noise doesn't have any inherent meaning or significance. In fact, your goal is to recognize it for what it is and move forward into a committed relationship anyway.

You wouldn't burn down your house because the air conditioner was too noisy. Likewise, you shouldn't sabotage or throw away a relationship because the silly voices in your head keep finding minor flaws with your new boyfriend. I promise you, you will miss those flaws when he's gone and no longer there. (Of course, if the voices in your head are telling you to burn down your home with your boyfriend inside, put this book down and call a doctor ASAP!)

Action Points

1) Tell Yourself it's Just Noise and Such Random Thoughts Are Meaningless

Remember, the noise is not a divinely inspired vision from the Grindr gods. It doesn't mean anything that your brain created a random thought or found a criticism. But as humans we don't train ourselves to realize just how much noise we make up in our heads. We usually conclude, "If I had this doubt, there *must* be something wrong. And if there is something wrong, then I should end things." But that's BS, and that mentality will kill off every relationship every time. So train yourself to recognize the difference between random noise and genuine issues you might have.

Ask yourself: *"Is this a genuine issue we're having or is this just stupid noise?"* 99% of the time you'll instantly recognize the difference. But for those instances where you're unsure, go back and look at your must-have list and your icing list. If the noise is centered around something on your must-have list, then you need to reflect on whether this guy can really meet your needs. But if it's not on that list, then chances are it's just random bullshit that popped into your head. So when you realize it's noise, actually tell yourself: **This is just random noise. It doesn't mean anything!**

The key is to get in a habit of constantly checking yourself, distinguishing the noise from the genuine issues. Most gay guys don't know the difference, so they will always be trapped. They think, "Why compromise on one guy when I can have ten more just like him?" Or maybe, "I can find someone hotter if I keep looking." The noise is never going to be happy no matter how perfect Prince Charming is, and it's never going to stop buzzing in the background—not unless you meditate, get into Zen Buddhism, and achieve "oneness." So unless you're gearing up to move to Tibet, the best you can do is start recognizing the noise for what it is: just background noise. Tell yourself that!

In Homer's Odyssey, Ulysses (aka Odysseus) was an ancient Greek warrior on a quest on a boat surrounded by seamen (sorry, I couldn't resist). Anyway, Ulysses' ship passed by the island of the Sirens: creatures who were half women, half bird, who would feed on the corpses of men; they would sing to seamen, luring them to approach their dangerous, rocky island. The Siren song would enchant the men (the straight ones anyway), and they would blindly steer their ships into the island cliffs, killing everyone on board and creating a meal for the Sirens. Your Grindr

Grief and commitment jitters can be as seductive as the Siren call. If you're not careful, you'll wreck a great thing, just to follow a stupid impulse. So resist, my friends! Resist! Ulysses had his seamen stick wax in their ears, so they couldn't hear. You just need to start training yourself to recognize (and resist) Grindr's Siren call.

2) Do NOT Act on the Noise

This should be obvious, but I'm saying it anyway. Do not take your internal noise as gospel, and do not do something foolish—like go onto Grindr and shag someone else because you didn't like your new boyfriend's mole. The main lesson in this commandment is to realize that often you should do nothing! Treat the noise as a wave in the ocean: let it wash over you, and let it recede back out into the void.

3) Tell Yourself: I'm Dating a Great Guy, and I'm Choosing Happiness in This Moment

Try actively telling yourself positive, uplifting things about your new guy and your relationship. You've been programmed your whole life to think that your random thoughts and feelings mean something to you and they're vital to keeping you safe. And even if you *theoretically* understand that many of your thoughts and feelings are irrational and silly, these thoughts and reactions still ***feel*** real in the moment, and you want to act on them accordingly.

Focus on the positives. Again, this is not Pollyanna-like naiveté, trying to convince yourself that everything in life is great when your life is in danger. If you're standing in a building that catches on fire, don't tell yourself to be thankful for the heat. Run out and call 911! But most of the time, we're not in emergency situations, but we react as if we were. So if you're dating a good guy who is genuinely into you, focus on that! Actively tell yourself: *I'm dating a great guy! He's trying to make me happy, and I'm embracing the happiness.*

Train yourself to accentuate the positives. For far too long, Grindr has given us so many options we could afford to focus only on the negatives. Cutting people off for BS reasons may be harmful in the long term, but it makes it a lot easier to figure out who you're going to meet on Saturday. Yet if you're looking to find something more substantial, you've got to flip this mentality around, and that takes practice. Actively remind yourself of all the good reasons why you're dating this guy: he's smart, he's funny, he's caring, he's great in bed! (You can mention the superficial stuff too; just focus on the positives.)

4) Ask Yourself: Is This Guy Worth One Month?

If you're still unclear as to whether you're dating a great guy with real potential, or whether you're just going through the motions, ask yourself: *Is this guy worth one month of my time? If I date this guy exclusively for one month, is it really the end of my world? Would dating him for four to six weeks really hurt my future prospects?*

99.99% of the time the answer to this question is obvious. On some level, he must have a few good qualities if you're even considering deleting Grindr, Scruff, Hornety (and the other apps) for him. Even if it ultimately doesn't work out, you probably need a break from the gay scene—or the gay scene may need a break from you, you big slut! So give this guy a chance. Invest some time and energy and don't let your fear of commitment sabotage a good thing!

Don't get upset if in reading this section, you see that you've self-sabotaged numerous times, believing your internal noise is gospel (or violating any of the other commandments). It's natural. It's human nature. And now you'll know better for the future. But I have a feeling that if you've read this book so far, and you've genuinely considered my positions and you're now taking action, you'll know the difference between silly thoughts that pop into your head and genuine deep issues that might jeopardize your relationship. Something inside of you has probably clicked. You've gotten tired of the same old shagging cycle. You're up for more, and you know how to make it happen. You get to say how your relationships get to go. You get to determine how people treat you. And you get to choose whether to be in a relationship or not. Just make sure you're not throwing something good away because the noise of trivial criticisms got in the way. Acknowledge that it's there, but love your new boyfriend—and his ugly moles—anyway. Something great is ready to happen to you! Just don't get in your own way. Just remember:

The Noise Doesn't Mean Anything! Let it Pass!

Commandment Summary: The Grindr Code: Live By it!

So now that you know my Grindr Commandments, live by them! Feel free to adapt any of them (except being flakey), but live by your own code. Stop letting random thoughts and base impulses dictate your behavior. Hold yourself to a higher standard than the code of Sleeping Beauties and Mindless Shag Zombies. To make this easier, I'm including a summary of the commandments without "Shalt" and "Shalt Not" language. And I'm including the action points!

1. **Don't Act Like a Douche**
   - Don't be unnecessarily mean online
   - Don't belittle others for not being your type
   - Try the Douchebag Test: ask a friend about a situation where you acted like a jerk but tell them that the other guy did it to you
   - Make Amends to those you've been a douchebag towards
     - If they are still upset, man up and let them vent
     - You'll feel better about yourself afterwards and you'll be more open to finding something new and great

2. **Be Responsible For Your Own Dating Life**
   - Don't be a Victim
     - Accept that you are responsible for whom you date and whom you choose to pursue
   - Make changes that empower you and bring you confidence—both external and internal

3. **Stop Seeking Perfection**
   - Open Yourself Up to Others who aren't your ideal type

4. **Know Yourself**
   - Distinguish what you *Must Have* in a relationship from what you can live without
     - There will be superficial qualities in this, and that's okay
   - Acknowledge that you let some good guys slip through your fingers, because you weren't truly committed to finding a great boyfriend

5. **Engage in Real Conversation**
   - Find out about the other person
   - Ask lots of questions
   - Don't give one or two word responses
   - Don't be afraid to ask someone out on a date or ask for their number
     - Remember: if he's not keen to text you back, he's not going to be keen to be your boyfriend

6. **Don't Be a Time Waster**
   - If the other guy isn't keen, let him go
     - A few times a year, invoke the *pretzel clause*. Do some minimal extra chasing sometimes, but only if he's super-hot
   - If you're not that keen to be with a guy that's chasing you, let him go
     - Put him out of his misery so he can find someone else who will love him just the way he is

7. **Don't Be Flakey**
   - NEVER flake out on someone or stand them up
   - Honor your promises—even the little ones
     - If you can't commit to small things like a first date, you're not training yourself to keep bigger commitments in serious relationships
     - Flaking out on people affects your consciousness in small ways you don't realize
   - If you think you may need to cancel, let the guy know ASAP
     - If you have to cancel, make an effort to reschedule

8. **Judge a Man by his ACTIONS, Never By His Words**

9. **Don't Let Rejection Rob You of Your Joy**
   - Accept that the majority of gay men won't be your soulmate
   - Stay upbeat despite rejection and mismatches
   - Stay unique and quirky

10. **Don't Listen to Fearful, Sabotaging Thoughts**
    - Fear of commitment and other negative thoughts do NOT have any inherent meaning
        - Just having a negative thought does NOT mean that something is wrong with you, your boyfriend or the relationship
        - Negative thoughts will pass; let them go
    - All humans fear commitment; don't sabotage yourself
    - As a gay guy, you will miss Grindr (and the dopamine highs you get from online flattery)
    - Train yourself to identify the noise in your head
    - Focus on the positives of the guy you're dating
        - Realize that dating this guy for a month or two isn't going to slow you down in the long-run

So there you have it ladies and gentlemen... Well, gentlemen... Actually, most of you bitches aren't even gentlemen.

There you have it, *fellas*! This is your new code. Live by it. And to the extent that one or two of these don't apply to you, feel free to adapt them. The main thing is for you to hold yourself to a higher standard.

My ultimate goal is to go online and see a hot gay guy taking a shirtless selfie and holding this book in his hand. Yum! Maybe I'll use that as a marketing ploy.

Hmmm...

Oops… I just did! LOL![8]

But joking aside, it's my hope that enough gay men start having these types of conversations and then find a way a way to let each other know. I admit it might look a bit corny if you read on someone's Grindr profile: "Hey guys. Just to let you know I'm worth investing in. I work on myself. I grow and develop. I treat people with respect, and I'm looking for something more." I would love it for people to start doing that, but I understand the fear of looking too desperate. So maybe we can get something trending on Twitter and Instagram that sends the same signal but doesn't look needy:

#GrindrCode, #GrindrCommandments, or #GayCommandments

---

[8] Why y'all gagging though? Yes, that's a real person, holding an actual copy of my book. He sent it to me on Instagram, and I happily added it to the latest version with his permission. Is it a bit cliché? Maybe, but he's hot.

If people who read this book start adding these hashtags to their profiles, it will get gay guys thinking. Yes, it might increase my book sales, but let's be honest. No nonfiction writer makes serious money from writing books. I'd make far more money being a partner in a law firm. Nothing pays the bills like mergers and acquisitions. But the key is for gay men to start forcing conversations of reflection, growth, better behavior, community and relationships onto the app scene.

I've been waiting for Lady Gaga or Elton John to descend from the Mountain top of West Hollywood to give gay men a code to live by and a better way to treat each other. But it hasn't happened. So all I can do is lift my own voice and ask others to do the same. If enough people get involved to do something as small as commit to adopting a few of these commandments, we'll all be a lot happier.

By the way, if someone comes up with a better way for gay men to elevate the conversation and behavior on dating apps, feel free to let me know. I'm happy to include those responses in this book (or future books). But for now, as I don't see anything else, let's just stick with these two hashtags. If you put this on your profile, and people ask about them, feel free to tell them. You don't even have to mention that you got it from this book. You can just say "It's a set of rules that a certain number of gay men are discussing in order to improve how we treat each other online." (But I certainly would appreciate it if you shared the book with them.)

Again, the key is to get our community talking and engaging rather than just mindlessly moving from shag to shag while hoping for a different result. If you live from something better, you'll attract others with the same mentality. And wouldn't it be great to know that when you approach someone online, and he's posted "I'm a Grindr Survivr who's now living by the #GrindrCode," or, "I follow the #GrindrCommandments," or something similar, you'll instantly know that he's been working on himself and he's open to more than the average Shagging Zombie or Sleeping Beauty.

On the other hand, if you're happy being a slut, then acknowledge that, own it, and enjoy it for however long that phase lasts. Don't lead people on and don't suffer over what a relationship could be if you're not really that committed to it. Accept where you are in your journey and enjoy it.

The gay community will never get better unless you decide to do something about yourself first. You can't force other humans to grow, but you can be part of something that sparks a conversation to help gay men live happier, more meaningful lives.

Part III:
General Tips, Guidelines,
& Recommendations

So finally, you got to the part of the book where I give you basic tips, recommendations, and guidelines on surviving in the age of online apps. I put this at the back of the book because I wanted to encourage the gay community to spend some time reflecting on why Grindr and other dating apps aren't making us happy. We need to reflect on why we treat each other terribly. If you just got a few tips on spotting fake profiles or taking a better selfie, then you'd be deceived into thinking your Grindr problem may be solved. But now that you've engaged in some solid introspection, and you're a more self-aware man, let's discuss some techniques for reducing the chances that you'll be tricked or manipulated.

Chapter One:
How to Navigate the Tinder Trap

I know this is a book about Grindr, but I had to say something about Tinder (and its gay counterpart Surge). In theory, the Tinder app could be the answer to all of our problems. It's clearly more relationship oriented than Grindr. It gives you more than one photo; you can link your Instagram account—even your favorite song on Spotify. You can write more text than you can on Grindr. Tinder requires you to have a Facebook account before you can use it, so there is a smaller chance of being catfished. And the Tinder app prevents you from sending direct photos to someone, which means it's impossible to get cock pics while you're eating your Cheerios. (Thank God!)

---

[9] I couldn't help but add this hilarious meme: original image source unknown.

Also, the matching function takes out a LOT of the drama that comes from Grindr. If a guy doesn't fancy you at all, he'll just swipe left. There's less risk of someone saying something nasty when you introduce yourself to a Tinder match. So in theory, Tinder leaves you with relationship-oriented guys who clearly find you attractive and are open to more than just sex.

In theory...

He'll like you on Tinder, but he won't message you!

Tinder vs. Grindr– It All Comes Down to Dopamine

In theory, Tinder should create so many relationships that it puts itself out of business. But remember, the technology is only as good as the people who use it. As much as I will complain about flakey guys on Tinder, I have to confess something about my own online dating habits. I get 90 to 95% of my dates from Tinder. Yet I spend more time on Grindr. Although I was getting fewer and fewer dates from Grindr, I continued to give it the lion's share of my dating app time. Dopamine fixes probably contributed to that.

Grindr allows anyone in your vicinity to send you a message. You can't stop their approaches—or the cock pics with your breakfast. And although you may hate the people who send that junk to you, we're easily addicted to the dopamine fixes or the flattery we get from someone throwing themselves at us, but we don't realize it.

Grindr will only keep you on their grid for one hour after signing in, so you have a constant incentive to check it frequently throughout the day. There's a thrill of mystery. You never know who's messaged you or what hot stranger may be down the street. Maybe it will be Prince Charming, although you know there's a 99.9999999999% it will be someone gross. But the hope from the lottery fantasy mixed with the constant flattery keeps gay guys coming back for more.

On Tinder, the "ugly people" can't contact you until you've swiped to match them. So off the bat, the average guy will eliminate receiving hordes of unwanted messages from "unattractive people." However, if that average gay guy is unknowingly addicted to the dopamine levels of Grindr, he'll always find Tinder lacking compared to Grindr. Tinder may feel like a letdown, so he won't use it as much. And because he doesn't use it as much, he makes it harder to find an emotional connection with those that do.

Match and Ignore

Perhaps, it's not a bad thing if everyone on Tinder entered it with a mind-frame of knowing that they were committed to dates or relationships. But I'd assert that many people on Tinder are still using it as a dopamine fix, although it never gives as much as Grindr. Many people use it for several reasons: (1) They enjoy passing judgment and rejecting people (swipe left) and deeming others worthy of contacting them (by swiping right). Tinder doesn't tell you who in advance likes your profile or not: you just make a judgment one profile at a time. So in that moment, you don't know for sure if the hot guy likes you, but you still get to pass judgment on him. (2) Gay guys get a dopamine injection from getting matches, but whether they realize it or not, they aren't open to anything more substantial. The result is hordes of cute guys on Tinder simply match people and never say anything; they simply ignore their matches.

Next to flakiness, I hate match & ignore—in part because the matching gives you hope that you've got a chance with a cute guy. But those hopes are quickly dashed when people say nothing. I wish I could track some of these people down and just scream, "WHY? What the fuck is wrong with you? If you don't fancy me, then fine, just swipe left." And of course, the first few lines of my Tinder profile say exactly this:

> *Looking for someone who looks at my profile and is up for grabbing drinks. The whole matching/ignoring thing is silly... But if that's your thing, feel free to swipe left.*

So I tell people, honestly, openly, I'm not here for your lame-ass swiping to get matches so you get a temporary ego boost. If you have 600 matches and no boyfriend, you have problems. But that's the mentality that pervades Tinder. No matter how hard I try, I have no advice on how to mitigate the scourge that is "match and ignore" on Tinder. You can be super great and keen to get to know the other guy, but he just uses it as a game.

Sometimes people do respond, but they take days because they check Tinder less frequently. So when someone says, "I never check this app," often he's indicating that he's too much of a Sleeping Beauty or a mindless Shag Zombie to be up for anything more. Because of the reasons I've laid out, new Tinder users quickly get disappointed and cynical about the app, because of the match & ignore or slow reply phenomena. So often new people who may be open to more than NSA just give up in disgust without investing any time into it.

Don't Be Afraid to Unmatch

When I first started using Tinder, I thought every match meant that every guy had read my profile and was open to dating me. Wrong! A match merely means that in one particular moment, some guy thought "cute enough" and swiped right. It doesn't mean anything more. The only strategy you can use is to save your own sanity. Accept the truth that most guys who swipe right for you aren't that keen to get to know you, so feel free to unmatch them so you can move on and chat to people who are keen.

I usually make two attempts to start a conversation, but if they don't respond, I unmatch and move on. That's all you can do. My conversation rule for Grindr applies even more so for Tinder: ***If they're not keen to chat with you on the app, then they're not going to be keen to be your boyfriend in real life.*** But I always at least make an effort on Tinder.

Always Start the Conversation

Too often, "shy guys" will never speak to each other because they are too afraid to say "hello" and make the first move. It takes ten seconds to type out, "Hey, how's it going?" So there's nothing stopping you. But remember, you might be a Piglet Paul, thinking you're a German model, so don't play hard to get. Get over yourself and conversate!

Sluts in Disguise

This isn't really a huge issue for me, but it's worth mentioning. A lot of Grindr sluts move to Tinder because they like the idea of sleeping with guys who are less slutty. I guess I can't be too mad at them; they're trying to steer clear of sexually transmitted diseases, but it's kind of funny that they want to act like sluts, but they don't want to do it with other sluts. That's why I've just started asking people pretty soon in the conversation, "So what are you looking for on here?" (And I've gotta point out the irony that for straight people, Tinder is as slutty as it gets. But for gays, it's darn near as chaste as a nun compared to other apps)

Get a Tinder Support App

Upgrade to Tinder Plus

Despite my complaints, I still think Tinder is vastly superior to Grindr, and I think it's a far better place to find a boyfriend. Just be braced for the realities of the app. Consequently, I think the upgraded features of Tinder Plus are totally worth it. In addition to unlimited "likes," Tinder Plus has a back-track/undo button that brings back your last swipe. This is crucial. Tinder is glitchy. Repeatedly, I will be swiping left to one guy, but as my finger is swiping, a different profile appears. The app often accidentally combines two profiles together, and if one of them is hot, you don't want to miss out.

Sometimes you can be mindlessly swiping left, trying to get rid of the ugly people in your town, but you're swiping so fast that by the time you come across a hot photo, your finger is moving faster than your brain can process. "Oh wait, he's cute." The Undo function on Tinder Plus is great.

Tinder has gotten greedy, and they're now charging something like $17 a month for Tinder Plus. That's highway robbery when it comes to apps, but it is worth it. Think of it as an investment in finding the right guy. More dates with good guys who are open to relationships are worth the extra money. And you save yourself more money by not going on as many lousy dates.

See Who's Swiped Right Before You Decide

There are loads of other apps that have "cracked" the code on Tinder; these apps connect to your Tinder profile, and they then show you exactly who else has swiped right in an attempt to match with you. You will usually have to pay for these apps, but they are worth every penny!

For me, my assessment of the person changes if I know that they have already swiped right. Again, you're going to have definite yes's and definite no's. But if you're undecided, knowing that the person has already liked you may make the difference. He's already keen, so why not.

See When They Were Last Online

Years ago, Tinder showed you when your matches were last active so you could tell whether the person was just ignoring you or just rarely using Tinder. But they stopped that, and I don't know why. This is vital when deciding whether to "Sashay Away" or waiting around for him to respond. But other Tinder support apps are still available to show you when your matches were last online. Again, don't be a stalker. Some people just take a bit longer to respond. But if he's constantly checking the app and not responding, then you know you need to unmatch.

Re-Set Tinder Every Four Months

A lot of people don't know this, but you can re-set your Tinder account. Doing this requires deleting your current account and then re-creating it. While that sounds like a pain, it actually only takes five minutes. After you delete your account, Tinder automatically gives you the option of re-starting it.

Of course, once you delete your app, then all of your current matches will disappear. And you'll have to go through the process of re-matching them if you want to chat again to them in the future. So before I reset my account, I just tell the guys I'm keen to meet and ask for their number. "Hey. I may delete this account in a few days, and I just wanted to see if you were up for swapping numbers." I've noticed that most of the time, faced with the option of losing a potential date, most guys say yes. So it's a great way to get other people to decide quickly whether they want to take things forward. (Also, if you had previously upgraded to Tinder-Plus, Tinder lets you reclaim your previous purchase at no cost.)

The process of re-matching with a guy shows whether he is keen to meet you. Remember the "New Jersey" singer who said he was looking for perfection? He, too, was hesitant at first. He never took the chat forward, which annoyed the hell out of me. But after matching with me three times, even he got that it was silly to keep matching with a guy and never taking it further. So we went on several dates. Ironically, he was super-hot, but I didn't care for his personality. It was a bit flat. And I think there was a let down on my part, after expending so much effort to get a hot guy to meet me, I was disappointed when rainbows and fireworks didn't shoot out of my ass when seeing him smile for the first time. But the continual re-match process did give me a date, so that might work for you too.

New and Revised Update!

Since publishing my book, I've had numerous friends come to me, asking for dating advice. Of course, these friends have never bothered to read my book. I suppose they're thinking, "Why read a book about dating when I can just get free customized advice from the author?" But putting my annoyance aside, I try to help them out. Remember Gloomy Grover from the introduction? Well, Grover came over to my place for a few drinks to have a catch-up. And as usual, he was whining about his lack of any boyfriend prospects. Remember, Grover is tall, blond, and very handsome, but he has no self-confidence. As he was grumbling, I was trying to see how he was sabotaging himself. My first question was, "Are you looking for relationships on Grindr or on Tinder?" Sheepishly and embarrassed, he explained that he was getting most of his dates from Grindr and Hornet. I gave him my infamous "Bianca Del Rio look," as if to convey that his explanation was moronic.

Grover then protested that he couldn't find a good match on Tinder. A tall handsome blond guy can't get a match on Tinder—gimme a break. I didn't believe it. So I challenged Grover to a test. I suggested we go through some Tinder swipes together, so I could analyze what he might be doing wrong. This led me to an amazing new insight. It was so eye-opening that I had to rush back and add this into my book, four months after publishing it. You could adapt this to Grindr or other apps, but it's especially applicable to Tinder, Surge, or any type of app where you have to swipe right or swipe left.

Action Point: Say Out Loud Your Reasons for Swiping Left or Right

In order for me to analyze Grover's decisions, I needed to know what he was thinking. So I told him to articulate out loud why he was choosing to swipe left or right. What came out of Grover's mouth was shocking.

"Oh no. He's wearing a flannel shirt," Grover said about one hot guy.

"Are you insane?" I protested, "The guy is hot."

"Yeah, but he's wearing flannel. Come on."

I tried to explain how ridiculously superficial this was, but Grover was completely oblivious.

Another ridiculous reason was, "No, that guy's profile has too many selfies. That can't be good. He must not have any friends." Again, I erupted at the sheer stupidity of that logic. But in Grover's mind, he thought too many selfies was a perfectly legitimate reason to swipe left. He looked at me as if I were the crazy one for insinuating that his thinking was anything less than Spock-like logic. I insisted that Grover was inventing a negative interpretation and cutting himself off from good potential dates for the silliest of reasons. But he just wouldn't compute that possibility.

Some of Grover's swipes were down to his particular type. Grover is 6'1", so he likes tall guys. But many of his reasons were stupid. He was complaining about not being able to find a boyfriend, but was literally inventing reasons to push cute guys away—like selfies or flannel shirts. I tried to get him to see that with such rigid standards, he was never going to find someone. But he refused to let the good advice sink in.

Grover became defensive and annoyed. I'm willing to bet that you're a tad less resistant than he is. The key is to say your reasons out loud. As you're saying things out loud, you're going to see aspects about your personality that aren't pretty. You're going to see how prejudiced you might be. You might see how superficial you are when it comes to body types. You may also see how just plain stupid your mentality is when it comes to dating. If you want a boyfriend, you're going to have to be in the right headspace, and nixing people for fashion choices is going to ensure you're single for a long time to come.

Bonus Points: Say Your Reasons Out Loud to a Friend

Moreover, saying your reasons out loud in front of a friend will REALLY expose who you are. In Grover's case, he was oblivious to how superficial he was being, but he was also a tad embarrassed at the same time, so part of him knew he was being ridiculous, although he didn't want to admit it in front of me. But when you say something out loud, and you can see someone's reaction, then you'll know whether you're being ridiculously picky. If your friend is constantly giving you the Bianca Del Rio look, then you know you're being a moron. It might not feel good, but you need to deal with it. If you don't want to be single for your entire life, you have to confront the parts of yourself that are not perfect.

Now, I'm not saying you can't have a certain "type" of guy. But remember Commandment IV, where I discuss distinguishing what you want versus what you must have. If you're swiping left because of silly things like too many selfies in a Tinder profile, chances are you're sabotaging yourself because that requirement was not on your must-have list. But if there is any confusion, saying your reasons out loud in front of a trusted friend is exactly what you need to help you decide.

The Greatest Irony in Online Dating

So, as per usual, Grover asked me for dating advice, and then promptly rejected everything I had to say. As a lawyer, I wanted to argue even argue against that level of defensiveness, which probably wasn't helpful to the situation. But as Grover and I continued this exercise, he said something else that caught me by surprise.

"Oh, I don't like his body. He's too skinny." I cocked my head to the side and gave Grover another Bianca look. Grover is very handsome, but he too is stick thin. He's like a handsome beanpole. I said, "Wait a minute, Grover. You don't have any muscle, but you're throwing shade at another guy for being skinny. Really?" Let he who has a perfect body cast the first stone.

Grover looked at me as if I had just murdered his pet puppy. He looked crushed. "But Andrew, that's not fair." "Yes, it is! It's perfectly fair. You're judging people on their bodies, so why shouldn't others judge you by the same standard," I said.

Grover then gave me a litany of excuses as to why he didn't work out: he didn't have time; he was stressed about his exams; he was trying to find a new job; he had had some family issues, blah, blah, blah.

I wasn't buying it. "So, Grover, you want people to have sympathy for the difficulties you're experiencing, but you have no sympathy for what anyone else is going through." He tried to protest this, but I quickly reminded him that he had just swiped left for a guy for wearing a flannel shirt.

Therein lies the entire irony of the gay community on apps.

On dating apps, we have a tremendous amount of sympathy for ourselves. We love to assuage our own egos with excuses as to why we may not be where we want to be in life—whether it's our level of fitness, our career, or our relationships. But we have zero sympathy for anyone else out there in cyber space. We judge them instantly on their photos and if anything is slightly off, they get a left-swipe or a block.

We want people to get to know us for the "real" us. We want a handsome prince charming to look beyond our flaws and see the beauty in our personalities, but we refuse to extend that same courtesy to anyone else who isn't super-hot.

And you wonder why you're still single, lol.

My conclusion about Grover was simple: he's a Slutty Sleeper. He likes being slutty, but he doesn't want to accept that about himself. So he tells himself how much he really wants a boyfriend, but just can't seem to find the right guy. I said, "Grover, your actions speak way louder than words. Your actions demonstrate that you have no interest in dating someone seriously because you keep shooting down all your potential suitors." Now he was really agitated. He protested, but of course, I shot down all of his bullshit excuses, which only made things worse. The last thing someone wants is for you to rip off their pretty little façade that they've been using to delude themselves for years.

I then realized Grover didn't really want my advice or my opinion. He just wanted me to confirm what he already thought: that all gay men were evil, and he was an innocent victim of mean, stupid gays. But giving my friends feigned sympathy isn't my strong suit. I gave Grover the truth, but he didn't like that. He was a bit annoyed with me for the rest of the evening, so I tried to change the subject and talk about other things, but I could tell my words had struck a nerve. Grover gave me some tremendous insights that day, but I was worried that in the process, I had damaged our friendship.

I didn't hear from Grover for a few days after that, and I was worried, as we normally text every day. I texted him reassuring messages, and he claimed to be fine, but I wasn't so sure. But about a week later he texted me: "I think you were right about me and relationships."

Hallelujah!

After that Grover began to just embrace that he didn't want anything serious. And I told him that was okay. Do what makes you happy. Grover just likes to suffer and be gloomy. And my point was, "cut the crap and embrace where you're at."

Ironically, a few weeks after that, Grover came to me asking for advice again. He had met a nice guy, and he was considering dating him exclusively, but he was nervous about making the commitment. "Ugh. Why don't my friends just read my book," I thought to myself. But I explained Commandment X: "Don't Listen to the Noise. Ignore all of those little thoughts that shoot the guy down. Just date him, enjoy his company for a while, and see how it goes." Surprisingly, he took my advice. It's early in this new venture for him, but he seems to be happy.

This all came from Grover's sharing out loud his reasons for crossing people off his list, and my taking the risk to give him honest feedback. Sharing things out loud with a trusted friend can really make a difference in helping you identify your own blind spots—areas where you sabotage yourself but you can't see it. That can make all the difference when you're trying to survive the crazy world of online dating.

Chapter Two:
Do You Look Like Your Photos?

At first, I debated whether to make this a commandment. This one seems so obvious, that it shouldn't need to be a commandment. This isn't really about self-growth, and yet I couldn't have a book about online dating without explaining some of the difficulties in moving from cyberspace to the real world. Usually, if people don't look like their photos, one of two things has occurred. First, they have tried to deliberately deceive you (which I'll address later). But more often, people are just using a good photo that's a few years too old or they're continually taking photos from their one good angle, which makes them look like a movie star when in reality they couldn't get cast as an extra for *The Walking Dead*. I've actually been on both sides of this equation, so all I can do is share my experiences.

There was this guy, let's call him Paul. Paul and I would chat on and off for ages—literally a year. He would always respond, but he was always playing hard to get. We'd chat for a bit, but we'd never try to meet. He had really cute photos, but what I never realized is that they were always from the same angle. Well, he clearly wasn't that interested, but I couldn't take the hint. I kept flirting and asking, and I finally got him to agree to meet me for a date. Foolishly, I had promised to buy the drinks. He was a poor student, and I wanted to show him what a great guy I was.

We agreed to meet at a subway station. And as I approached, I spotted him from a distance, but he hadn't yet seen me. My reaction was instant. Never in my life has the online presentation looked so different from the in-person view, and that includes the times I was catfished! He was clearly the same person from the photos, but he looked nothing like his pictures. Like nothing! Paul looked like Piglet from *Winnie the Pooh*! Paul was not obese but from the shape of his nose, ears, and head, he looked somewhat like a pig. He was kind of cute in a Piglet sort of way, but he definitely wasn't for me.

As you guys know, I don't flake out on people, and I would never stand someone up. But when I saw Piglet Paul in person, I wanted to run away like Usain Bolt. I almost did. I turned around, but I thought "No, that's just rude, particularly if you asked him out." Part of me felt like he deserved it, though. I wanted to run away and text him, "Hey asshole, next time don't make me wait a year." But I didn't do that. I took Piglet Paul out for a few drinks—such a waste of money, but we had a polite conversation, and that was that. But the instant I was out of ear-shot, I called my sister and moaned to her for more than an hour. "Oh, the humanity."

My poor sister had to deal with 60-70 minutes of non-stop melodrama. I explained ad nauseam that it wasn't just the fact that he didn't look like his photos; it was that he made me jump through so many hoops to meet him. He played so hard to get that when I saw the real thing, I was like, "What? Oh, Hell No! That little wannabe Piglet made me jump through hoops for a year and for what?!?!" I expended so much effort and energy all for nothing!"

If he had sent realistic photos and he had asked me out on a date, then maybe that would have been different. The very notion that he thought that meeting me was somehow doing me a favor! Ugh. I realized I was thinking, "How dare that Piglet Paul think he's hotter than me?!" My ego was bruised more than anything else. I had foolishly wasted loads of time and effort on a lost cause, rather than just "cutting it off" and moving on. It was my own fault for barking up the wrong tree, and yet he looked NOTHING LIKE HIS PHOTOS.

After screaming at my sister for an hour, who very graciously took the tongue lashing that was meant for Paul (don't worry, she laughed the entire time), I went back and looked at Paul's Instagram profile. They were all taken from the same two angles. All of them! Not one deviated from those two angles. Of course, now that I had seen him in real life, I saw nothing but the "pig" contours in his face. "How could I have been so stupid?!" His face to this day sends chills down my spine. Not because he's the ugliest person on the planet, but because it just reminds me of how deceiving photos can be and how stupid I was to waste so much time on someone who was never that keen on me to begin with.

Tip: Look At Instagram

One of the biggest tools in deciphering how someone really looks is to examine their Instagram page. People always let a few "real" pics slip onto their page. And don't forget to check the tab to see where their friends have tagged them. These photos will give you enough of an idea of what the guy will look like. But I admit that this is not foolproof. Not everyone has Instagram, particularly guys over 35. You can ask for Facebook, but that looks creepy. You can still look them up on Facebook (sometimes you can identify them using their phone number) and look at their profile pictures to get a better idea of what they might look like. But certainly don't add them to your Facebook at this stage.

If they say they don't have Instagram and they are under 30, chances are they are lying. They may be catfishing you, or they could just not be on that app. But either way, be cautious if they don't have Instagram. Be prepared for the fact that they may not look anything like the photos you've seen.

Dodgy Lighting Made Me a Super Hero

But don't worry, I've been on the other side of that Piglet scenario. A few years ago, I was taking a post-gym selfie in my flat. The lighting was weird. It was cloudy that day, so little sunshine was coming in, and the overhead lights weren't very bright. So I just turned on the flash on my camera. I don't know what happened, but that flash worked a miracle. Somehow with the low lights and the flash, I looked like a movie star! Photography isn't my field of expertise, so I can't begin to explain it, but I looked hot. My muscles looked bigger. My face didn't have any flaws. I looked AMAZING!

I threw those photos up on the internet, and I got a response. I arranged to meet up with a super-cute German guy who was also a model. (You know how this is going to end.) Well, as first dates go, it wasn't as bad as some. But when he walked in, I could tell he was disappointed. I went to the bathroom to see if I could spruce myself up at all. But what the hell can you do in the men's toilet of bar. I didn't have any hair gel, and my face was my face: it's not like I had some spare Botox in my pocket. All was lost. My confidence was shot, and that was that.

I was surprised when he texted me a few days later. He just started chatting like it was nothing. I was suspicious as to what he was after, but I kept the conversation going. Eventually, I asked him if he wanted to meet up again. He made clear that he loved my personality, but he just wanted to be friends—like "no sex, ever" were his exact words. So yeah, he liked me but not enough to sleep with me. Imagine how I reacted to that. The fangs came out.

I told him off for wasting my time and giving me false hope. But at the very least it confirmed to me that it was merely my appearance that threw him off. This happened one more time shortly thereafter. And I realized it was likely my super-hero photo. It was "too hot" relative to me in real life. So as much as I hated to, I stopped using those pics.

If the first thing that someone feels when they see you is disappointment, that's a hint and a half to get different photos. Now me, having experienced piggy-boy and been turned down by the German model, I just started sending different photos to friends: "Do I look too hot in this photo? Is it unrealistic?"

Some of you may laugh at this, but you're wondering why the hot guy doesn't call you back. It's because you keep photo-shopping out all of your bad skin and acne scars. (I had that happen to me too not too long ago.) #SorryNotSorry. We all know we put our best photographs on dating apps, particularly Grindr, which only allows you one photo.

Some of you might be thinking, "Well, at least you got them to meet you for a date." But so what? First impressions matter. And if their first impression is disappointment, or they feel deceived or tricked, then they're not going to view you as boyfriend material. Not even a winning personality like mine can recover from that initial disappointment.

Alternatively, some of you might be thinking, "Well, guys shouldn't be that superficial." Yes, in an ideal world, you'd be correct. But in an ideal world, Trump wouldn't be president. People are people. And if you are purposefully using only one angle or are actively concealing elements of your face, then you're trying to deceive someone without being responsible for the potential consequences of disappointment. So I could pronounce: **Thou Shalt Look Like Your Photos**, but that's a tough call, particularly if you are really photogenic. So rather, let me say this: find some friends who will be honest with you and ask them directly:

Is this photo an accurate representation of me? Do I look "too hot" in this pic?

Better a friend tell you the truth than you spend months or years wondering why no one ever calls you back.

Tip: Get Someone Else to Take Your Photo

"What if I'm not photogenic?" You might be asking. I certainly fall into this category. Then, in that case, get a friend who is an amateur photographer and take loads of photos—like 100 maybe 200—just to get one good shot. I've noticed a difference with me. I always look better if they're using a real camera and not just a smart-phone. While camera phones are getting better, they can distort your face in close proximity, and they may not be right for you. Certainly, the "selfie" camera in the front almost never produced a good photo (until I got the iPhone 6, and even then I have to take 100 to get two good ones). So ask around and see if you can find a friend to take a few decent photos of you.

I asked my friend Size Queen Simon to come over and take pictures of me. We had good lighting outside, and he got some great shots. I didn't look super hero hot, but I still looked good, and I got a lot of dates out of those pics. It was well worth the pizza and beer I bought Simon to say thank you. I told him jokingly, "Never in my life has one man's intervention had such a direct impact on getting me laid. Thank you!"

Or you can hire a professional photographer, but that can come across as looking creepy or looking like a "wannabe" model or trying too hard if a professional photographer puts you in weird clothing or takes photos of you half naked in the middle of a busy street. The point is not to be afraid to ask for help in getting a better photograph. Yes, it seems like energy and effort, but every gay man you message online will judge you by that photo, so make sure it's good, yet realistic.

If paying a dude $100 bucks for an hour seems like a waste of money, then ask yourself if you get five good photos (which are both realistic and hot), which leads you to getting four or five dates with hotter people, then is it then worth it?

As Tatiana from Drag Race says, "Choices."

It's tough balancing hot with realistic. There will always be a big incentive to make that photo as good as possible. But if people are seeing you and then running away screaming, you need more realistic photos. On the other hand, if you're going to ignore my good advice and you continue to use your photo-shopped pictures, then you better be the nicest guy in the world. At the very least, make it easy for your dates to reject you after meeting you. Meet them in their area of town. Buy ALL of the drinks. Ask lots of questions. Don't be like Piglet Paul and make them jump through endless hoops only to find out that you're not as hot as you led them to believe. No one deserves that.

A Quick Note on Profile Text

One thing I always suffer over is profile text. As I mentioned before, 95% of the time, it will NOT matter, particularly on Grindr. Most guys don't care about your intelligence, your personality, or your heart if they aren't already attracted to you—unless you have a job that might be useful to them—like being a talent scout for a record company. That being said, you should still write something. It will be icing on the cake to people who are into you, so make the cake as tempting as possible.

Profile text can do several things:

- Explicitly state what you're looking for (i.e., relationship, dates, NSA)
- Say something about yourself
    - Job
    - Education
    - Hobbies
- Stand out from the crowd by saying something funny.

A totally blank profile looks suspicious to me, and now it will look suspicious to all my readers. In Commandment V: Thou Shalt Conversate! I explain how you might want to indicate what you're looking for. But you should say a few things about yourself.

If you have a good job, such as being a doctor or a lawyer, go ahead and put that out there. While icing on the cake, it signals to people that you're worth investing in because you're educated and successful. Ironically, I've met loads of asshole bankers and slutty doctors. But it's still prestigious. The issue I find is that I'm super smart and successful, and I've been told more than once that "I'm bragging." Sometimes that's just what some insecure queen tells me because he dropped out of high school. But beware:

Guys are intimidated by people who are significantly smarter and more successful than they are.

Not all gay guys feel this way, but a lot do. In fact, I have to put myself in that camp. Because I went to Harvard, I'm used to being the "smart one" in the relationship. And on occasion, when I meet someone smarter than I am, it is a bit intimidating. It makes me question, "What am I adding to this potential relationship?" We're all really quirky about what we offer and what we hope to get out of a relationship. So I freely admit that I do the same thing I find annoying in other people, but at least I'm honest about where I'm a hypocrite. But I digress….

Tip: Tamp Down Your Success, Pivot to a Passion

So how do you signal in your profile text that you're a cut above the rest, but not look like an arrogant asshole? Briefly mention your job, but don't go into great detail. Don't tell people you're the richest banker on Wall Street or that you perform brain surgery every day. Just mention your profession casually and then instantly pivot to your passion or a hobby that more people can relate to:

- Pediatrician who enjoys cycling and bad TV.
- I work in finance, but my real passion is art.
- Lawyer by day; Ninja assassin by night.
- Accountant who has a sense of humor—Have you heard the joke about the bear taking a shit in the woods next to a rabbit?

You're free to poke fun at yourself or your profession. Obviously, if you're able, say something funny or steal something funny you saw someone else write in another city. (Don't steal the profile text of the Grindr guy down the street.) Humor helps, although I'm crap at writing funny things down (as you just saw above). But the key is don't be afraid to send potential partners a signal that you're a cut above the rest; just stay relatable. Try not to come across as intimidating or arrogant.

Tip: Avoid Obnoxious Profile Text

On the flip side, people write loads of offensive and rude comments on their profile text. Usually relating to types of physical attributes that they don't want. I refer you to my comment on douchebaggery. You may think you're being cute or you're ferreting out people whom you would never date, but I promise, obnoxious remarks will turn off good people who are cute and have kind hearts. My friend Size Queen Simon is white, and he dates all races, but he once told me that he'd never date a white guy who wrote something racist on his profile. That kind of arrogance or lack of sensitivity is a turn-off to him. Again, you can't help whom you fancy, but tact goes a long way.

Chapter Three:
How to Spot Fake or
Deceptive Profiles

One of the many problems with Grindr and online dating is the ability of certain men to steal photos from hotter men and try to catfish the rest of us into meeting them. I believe that this is a big problem in the gay community, although it must be a big enough problem in the wider straight community for MTV to make a show about it. It's scary and revolting when someone shows up, and they don't look like their photos. They're hoping you won't notice the difference, and hey, what do they have to lose? They were going to get rejected anyway. They're hoping that you're either too stupid to tell the difference or you're already so emotionally invested in meeting them that you'll give them a chance.

As I already proclaimed, "Thou Shalt Look Like Your Photos!" But there is a big difference between people using a five year old photo or a "glamor shot" that's been enhanced with an Instagram filter or photo-shopped and people using photos of an entirely different person.

I have to say that I've gotten fairly good at spotting fake profiles and would-be catfishers. And since this book is about navigating online dating and surviving apps like Grindr, avoiding fake or deceptive profiles is a major piece of this. These aren't hard and fast rules, so think of these as guidelines or potential warning signs. One by itself may not be a big deal, but three or four should be a red flag!

Beware the Blank Profile!

It's cliché to moan about the numerous torso shots on Grindr, and yes, it makes us all too superficial. But at the same time, on occasion I've turned Grindr on while I was near a business environment. And I certainly wouldn't want that gossipy old queen at work seeing me shirtless on any dating apps—and every office has that one gossipy queen who's into everyone's business. (Half of the people reading this are probably that gossipy queen.) News of your six-pack will be all over the office in two seconds flat. For this reason, I don't blame people for not showing their faces if they're not out at work or don't want to be seen as "grinding" near the office.

However, that being said, a sure-fire sign that something is wrong is when you get a message from a cute guy and his main profile is totally blank, as in no face, no torso, nothing. That's always a major warning sign that you might be being catfished.

Why? Although I certainly can't prove it, because catfishers won't exactly be open and honest with me, I strongly suspect that guys who use a totally blank profile are actually exploring the option of cheating on their boyfriends. And trust me, these guys are paranoid as hell. They're testing the waters as to whether they can do better than their current boyfriend, and they don't want to get caught.

These guys, I suspect, don't even use sunsets or landscapes as their Grindr photos for fear that someone will recognize the landscape from social media. If you've just taken a bunch of beautiful sunset photos in Spain with your boyfriend, and you've posted them to Instagram and Facebook, you'd probably be too scared to use one of them as your Grindr profile, because a friend might recognize the photo and tip off the boyfriend.

They're probably too scared even to use a headless torso shot. If a guy has a boyfriend, he's probably scared to show off his chest, for fear that a mutual friend or acquaintance might see it, recognize the torso, and alert the boyfriend. So when someone messages me online and their profile is completely blank, then that's a RED FLAG! Watch Out! Buyer Beware!

I once got a message from a guy on Grindr. He told me he was from "New Jersey"—instant red flag—and to make matters worse, he had a completely blank profile. Realizing that this is a massive risk, I asked about it. He explained that he was a teacher, and so he had to be careful about using a hookup app when he's responsible for small children. Fair enough, I thought. He did have several other pics to send, but he claimed he didn't have Instagram.

We chatted on WhatsApp for a bit and arranged a date. We confirmed on the day to meet that afternoon, but as I got to the meeting place, his profile pic on WhatsApp disappeared. (That means that the person has recently deleted the picture without replacing it, or he's completely blocked you.) I rang him to check, and suddenly "It has not been possible to connect your call." I stood there for fifteen minutes in shock. I knew what had happened, but I couldn't believe it. It was the only time in my life that I've been literally stood up—as in I was there, waiting at the designated meeting place and the guy simply didn't show up (rather than canceling via text shortly beforehand). I still get angry thinking about it. I was furious, but what could I do? Looking back, there was only one red flag. His Grindr profile was totally blank: no picture of him, his torso, or a landscape shot.

I don't know if he was stealing another person's pictures and using them on a completely separate phone. But I'm more inclined to think that he was trying to cheat on his boyfriend and got a sudden case of cold feet, regrets, doubts or something like that. Ever since then, I've been super cautious around guys with blank profiles. And it won't surprise you to learn that I have not had a date with a blank profile since. In fact, the last time someone even approached me online with a blank profile (but sent private pictures of a handsome man), I was able to question him to the point where he knew he was busted, and he got mad and blocked me. I didn't get angry or nasty. I just asked a few basic questions. He knew the jig was up, and he bolted.

So please try to learn from my mistakes so you don't have to be in that position. Be smart, ask questions, and then use your gut to see whether this person is worth your time.

Closet Cases Are a Red Flag

The other old chestnut of an excuse that catfishers throw out is "I'm not out." They usually use this excuse when you ask for more than one photo. The catfishers don't have any more to send, so they just make up an excuse. In some places, gay guys do have to be careful about being online. But this book isn't for closet gays in Tehran. This book is for gay guys living in large Western cities. And it's highly unlikely that a hot 30 year old appears super gorgeous in one photo but doesn't have any more pics because he's "not out yet." Use your brain; trust your gut. Analyze the whole situation, and if something feels funny, then something is probably wrong.

This is a very convenient excuse since we all have a "coming out" process. And it's not fair to judge someone who is at a different stage of this journey than you are. But catfishers know this, and they're happy to use it to their advantage. They're hoping that by saying, "I'm not out" or "I'm discreet," you won't press them for any more pictures or for other details that might reveal their mendacious tendencies that make it easier for them to trick you.

Age is usually a dead give-away online. If he's messaging you and claiming to be 30 but not yet out, then he's probably lying. More and more gay kids are coming out younger and younger. I'm not saying that no one ever comes out after 30. In fact, I have a good friend who came out at 50. But I'm saying that when people say, "I'm not out," it's a red flag, so be careful!

As a matter of course, I always ask to see someone's Instagram. And if some guy is giving you the "I'm not out" speech and can't share any details, then what he is likely communicating to you is: *I'm a dirty, ugly liar, and if I keep chatting, you'll figure this out. So best keep you in the dark, till I'm ready to make my move*. Trust me, hot straight guys LOVE to get gay followers on Instagram. Take this as a warning sign and trust your gut after chatting to him for a while.

Certainly snapchat is an option also. Those photos disappear. There's no harm in sending a few snaps just for verification purposes.

Examine the Background of the Photo for Clues

I've spent significant amounts of time in both Europe and America, so I've learned to spot the differences between bathrooms and bedrooms on both continents. I've noticed that in Europe lots of catfishers steal pics from American guys, but you may not be able to tell if you don't know the subtle differences in the background.

European bathrooms (and the homes containing them) could be built in many different time frames. Some of them are over 100 years old, and so the sinks and doors in the background will look very different. Also, European bathrooms tend to have towel heaters in their bathrooms whereas that's rare in the US.

Most American homes were built in the 50s and 60s. And so the bathrooms tend to have a similar look, particularly the sinks, the showers and the bathroom doors.

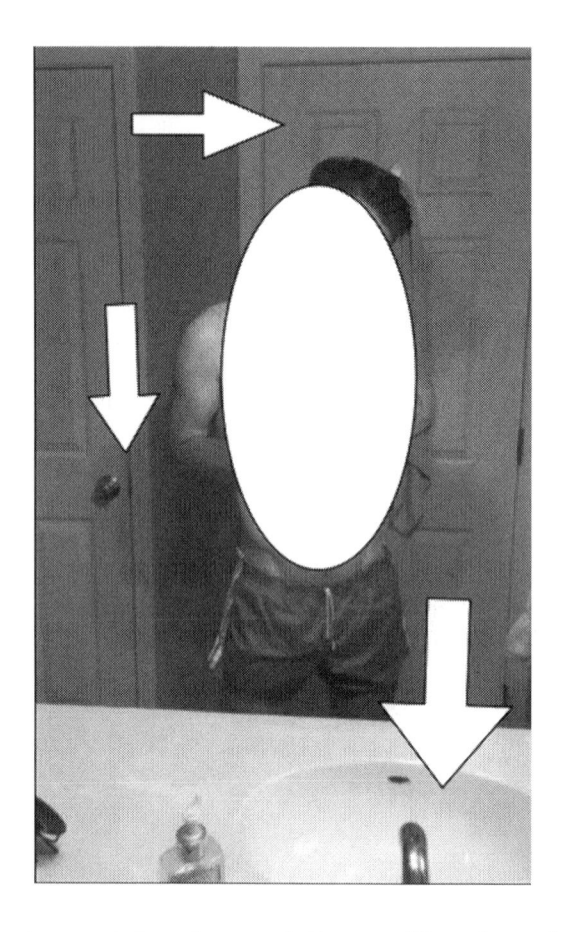

This photo was taken from a dating profile, where the alleged single man was Italian, as in actually from Italy. Now, Italy has some of the oldest architecture in the Western world. So it's highly unlikely that an Italian apartment would have brand new, wide wooden doors, American style door handles, and a modern sink (although some European sinks and bathrooms have had a recent makeover, so this particular sink is somewhat ambiguous).

American doors tend to be wider than European doors, and they tend to have the same style of indentation and carved patterns. The handles tend to be brass and round. European doors have a thinner, straight lever handle rather than a round knob or a curved lever handle. And usually European doors don't contain patterns; they are just a flat wooden surface.

This is a typical European bathroom door.

Also, many European bathtubs, built and designed 100 years ago, have a bathtub with a shower handle attached to the tub itself, not affixed above where the average human would stand. Again, this would be indicative of a European bathroom.

I'm not saying that no bathroom in Europe can have the same style as an American bathroom. I'm sure some of them are identical, but you get the point. There are differences between the two as a general trend. So if a super-hot guy doesn't have any more photos and you recognize a bathroom or bedroom style that is different from your home country, you're probably being catfished.

Also, be on the lookout for electrical plugs—they are small and in the background, but they are a dead giveaway. American plugs look completely different from European plugs (or mains as they are sometimes called).

Below is an American electrical socket.

Immediately below is a British socket.

And below is a continental European electrical socket.

Look for these plugs in the background of photos. If you're living in Idaho, and you notice a British plug socket in the background, then be suspicious. A few simple questions will reveal whether he's catfishing you. If you ask him where he's from and if he's done any international travel recently, then you can use this information in assessing whether he's catfishing you.

Short Conversation / Rushing to the Point

This is obvious, but catfishers know that they're lying. They know they're being slimy. So their number one fear for their behavior on the app is being reported or exposed. So in general your average catfisher is going to be evasive and edgy. That comes through in their online chat.

One could argue that apps like Grindr make us all rush a bit too fast to the bedroom, and we don't spend enough time getting to know each other as people. But usually when someone is trying to rush you into the sack, and they don't want to meet you for a drink first in a public place, they may be hiding something. This isn't an iron-clad rule. The guy might just be a dirty slut. But he might be edgy to get you to agree to hook up so he can show up on your doorstep and hope that you won't notice that he's not the guy in the photos.

"Are You Catfishing Me?" You'd be Surprised How Often This Works!

This is going to sound obvious, but not enough of us do it. Remember, these guys know that what they are doing is slimy and underhanded. In their ideal world, you will never wise up to the fact that you've been deceived until it's too late. If I see some troubling signs regarding their photos (or lack thereof), I sometimes just flat out ask, "Are you catfishing me?"

Now, I know what you're thinking: "He's just going to deny it." And you're right. In that moment the catfisher will lie and say, "Of course not. I'm just discreet." Or he'll use some stupid excuse like that. But the process of your asking him puts him on the spot, and it lets him know that you're not as easy to fool as other guys.

The majority of the time, once you ask, "Are you catfishing me?" the guy will instantly lose interest. He knows the jig is up. He'll deny it at the time, but he will later avoid or block you. Yes, your hopes will be dashed in the moment because you were falling in love with that gorgeous photo, but that outcome is far preferable to the ugly reality showing up on your door.

Use the tips I've shown you here and think carefully about a guy if he doesn't have any profile pic or is telling you that he's not out.

Deceptive Daddies and Bored Boyfriends

Look For an Old iPhone

Although not as traumatic as being totally catfished, it sucks when someone doesn't look like their photos because they sent you one from five years ago. Older guys love to pass off outdated photos to younger guys as a means to trick them into meeting.

So if a guy sends you a post-gym selfie, and he's on an iPhone 4 or a Blackberry, then you know the picture is five to ten years old. Or if it's super grainy, then you also know the picture is a five to seven years old. When a guy hits 30, things start to change: the metabolism slows and the wrinkles appear. So there can be a mountain of difference between 29 and 34. Don't get tricked!

Guys in Open Relationships

Sometimes, when a guy is super direct with you and uninterested in meeting for a drink or anything, these guys aren't necessarily catfishing you, but they have a partner, and they're not interested in anything with strings. That's not necessarily a bad thing—if they are being honest with you. This book isn't about judgment; it's about making an informed choice. What's happened to me more than once is that guys will **LIE** about being in an open relationship—or *conveniently* forget to tell you until after they've gotten what they're after.

Personally, I avoid guys in open relationships. I don't want to risk getting physical and feeling something for a guy I can never have. But that's just me. You're free to choose. But I think it's underhanded when they avoid telling you that they aren't single. They know that lots of single guys aren't cool with hooking up with someone that can't ever offer any real long-term dating potential, but they want to keep their options open. You may be looking for a future husband; he's just looking for an over-grown flesh-light to spice up his old relationship. And what does he care if you get hurt in the process?

If a cute guy messages me online, I usually check out his profile to ensure that he's single. And if it's blank, I definitely ask. Again, men—gay or straight—are slimy, and they're happy to use you or lead you on if it gets them what they want. So if you don't ask, he probably won't tell.

Chapter Four:
No More Coffee Dates
(And Other First Date Tips)

So I've come to a decision! Absolutely no more coffee dates ever (with one exception, which I'll mention later). Needless to say, I had a bad experience at a coffee shop. Well, it wasn't a bad experience, but it wasn't a great one either. I really liked the guy. I was moderately charming. I definitely wanted a second date, but despite the usual, albeit insincere, texts to meet up again, it never happened. I know I was the guy's type, but he never suggested a second date, so I left him alone. Maybe it just didn't click, but I can't help but think that the coffee shop killed the spark.

Because nice looking guys are inundated with offers, chances are you're only going to get one bite at the apple. The problem is for the stars to align, you need to really "click" with a guy. No pressure, but you better look your best, be funny, sound intelligent, sound confident (but not arrogant), listen intently, ask good questions, make the other guy feel special, and give him a kiss that makes butterflies swarm in his stomach. And don't say anything offensive or fucking stupid![10]

On some level, you just have to surrender to the simple truth that not every guy you meet is going to like your personality, and

---

[10] On my first date with Arnold the Architect, I once made a bad joke and used the word "retarded." I didn't realize that Arnold was a volunteer for special needs children... Awkward! My bad, by the way. He gave me a stern yet respectful lesson on why using that word isn't cool. I apologized, and after that everything was fine. But I've had other instances, where one wrong question or phrase has led to another "space ship explosion."

you'll likely find a lot of gay guys boring or annoying. That's just how it is. But that being said, you still want to put your best foot forward. You want to listen, engage in a good conversation, be funny, and see how things go.

Some dates will be great. Some dates will be awful. But some dates just go a bit "Meh." Nobody did anything wrong. You each thought the other was cute. Maybe you both intended to see each other again, but it just fizzled out afterwards. In these cases, it could be that it just wasn't meant to be, but I have another sneaking suspicion.

Your Dating Environment Matters!

Yes, on some level there needs to be a certain spark, and both guys need to think the other is worth seeing again. But I've come to the conclusion that such a spark can NEVER be kindled in a coffee shop. Ever! At least for me, it can't.

Coffee Shop Exception:

Now there is one set of circumstances, where I will suggest a coffee date with someone. This could get me into trouble, but I'll say it anyways. I'll suggest a coffee date if the guy isn't my type, but he's been extremely persistent. I know it's shady. But as I said, I want to try to stay open to people who are keen to get to know me, but if I suspect that he just can't be my type physically, the coffee shop is a safe bet. The dates are always the same: they're polite but never that exciting. So that way, the other guy is left without feeling a spark, so it's no big deal if I never call him back. In theory, if his personality blew me over the moon, then we could meet up again. But to date, that has never happened.

So just be mindful of the environments you choose to meet someone. Is it going to foster romance? Would you feel comfortable making a move there?

First Date: Always a Gay Bar

For me, I usually pick a gay bar that has space, a friendly environment, plenty of seating, and LOTS of red wine. I avoid straight bars or places where PDA would seem silly. And I also avoid places where it's going to be crowded or appear pretentious because that puts me on edge.

Think about it. You're meeting a stranger off of the internet. You don't know what his voice sounds like. You don't know what his personality is going to be like. You're praying to God he looks like his photos. And you have to be actively engaged in the conversation. That's stressful. I need a drink, damn it! A glass of wine helps me to be more relaxed, and I'm more inclined to make jokes. For me, laughing is an absolutely essential part of a good first date. So putting my alcoholism aside, what point am I making?

Your environment will definitely affect the mood of your date, and mood is key. So if you're keen on a guy, make sure he's relaxed and can have a few drinks!

Imagine this: you're in the park; it's warm and sunny. Your date brought a nice bottle of wine, maybe some cheese or chocolate. You're sipping wine, having nibbles, making each other laugh. He then leans in to kiss you....

Do you see how that environment enhances a feeling of romance?

Now imagine as he leans in to kiss you, you hear a thunderclap, and rain starts pouring down.

What's changed? The wine hasn't gone bad (rain won't hurt it). Your date is still hot. Hell, he may even be sexier now that he's wet. But chances are you'd be looking for a place to go inside because the rain sours the mood.

Now you don't have to plan an elaborate picnic date for every single guy you meet, but before meeting, you can ask yourself: "Will this environment help or hinder a spark." And for me, coffee shops are places sparks go to die. There's no alcohol. Depending on where you are, homosexual public displays of affection can be awkward—even dangerous in some parts of the world. So if I'm worried about whether it's appropriate (or safe) to kiss the guy, I probably won't make the move.

Always Kiss a Guy on the First Date

Almost without fail, if I don't get a kiss on the first date, it never goes anywhere. I can't really explain why, but a kiss is key to creating a spark—maybe because it brings out a primal instinct. But in any event, a lot's riding on that first kiss. If it feels organic and natural, that's going to contribute to his feeling a spark. If it's forced at the end or it doesn't happen at all, then he's less inclined to have romantic feelings. And a good kiss might be the difference between "Yeah, I'll see him again" or the obligatory "Let's hang out again soon," which never happens.

Kiss Him in the Middle of the Date

If you're keen on the guy, you must find a way to give him a smooch. But don't wait until the end of the date. At that point it feels awkward and forced: you're both kind of preparing for it, but it seems awkward. And by that point, he's probably concluded that there's no spark. You've gotta work the kiss into the middle of the date so there's still time to build on the spark if it pops.

Personally, I have never had a kiss backfire—in that it never made things super awkward or ruined the rest of the evening. He'll either feel a spark or he won't, but you're no worse off.

Pretend to Be Confident

Even if you're scared, **PRETEND to be confident!** This is the only time where I will tell you NOT to be yourself but to pretend to be something different. In this case, fake it till you make it!

Leaning in, locking eyes, and kissing brings out some of our primal urges. It's your way of showing that you think he's attractive and you're not afraid to show it. And even if he reacts in a shocked manner, you should "stay in character." In fact, if he's stunned, do it again! Let him know you're keen and confident. That's an attractive combination in person, but it's hard to demonstrate online.

Sit Strategically

Because you need to kiss him in the middle of the date, pick your seats carefully. In the spring and summer time, it's easy to sit outside. Often bars have outdoor tables where you can enjoy the sunshine. Avoid this. You can't kiss a guy across a table. *Find a seat where you can sit next to him as opposed to across from him.* Or if you've discovered that he's a Piglet in disguise, choose a seat where he can't lean in and kiss you.

Chapter Five:
Bring Your Kinky Boots

I haven't seen the musical *Kinky Boots* yet. I actually know a guy who's in it, but he still hasn't offered me a complimentary ticket—not even a 10% discount actually. But, oh well....

If you probably haven't guessed by now, this chapter ain't about a musical. Actually, I'm surprised that I haven't really addressed the topic of sex head on this book so far. On one level, if you're reading this book, you're probably not a virgin. But I suppose it couldn't be a book about Grindr and online dating if I didn't at least mention the topic of sex.

Part of the reason I hesitated to bring it up is that everyone's doing it, and if anything we need to bring some awareness (or "mindfulness" if we want to get Zen about it) to our sexual interactions, and the awareness needs to be gained *before* we're both naked in a bedroom because at that point critical thinking goes right out the window.

Conversely, I think some guys are on a bit of a high horse about slut shaming. The interactions themselves are just basic biology. As the Drag Queen said in the movie *The Crying Game*, "It's just a piece of meat." Sex on one level is just two pieces of meat attached to bodies that are huffing and puffing and rubbing and thrusting. The biological act by itself doesn't necessarily hold any intrinsic meaning. That doesn't mean that we should all go out and have meaningless sex. Sex can mean something. And I personally believe it's better when it is attached to love or an emotional connection.

The problem is that we're not having open and honest conversations about what sex means to us and how to improve sexual experiences and how we'll respond afterwards. Sometimes we don't want to give it out too freely, and other times we just want a shag to get through the week. Gay men go back and forth in terms of their wants, but we act out all too easily on our baser instincts. So here are some questions we should pose to ourselves in the areas of sex before we hook up with someone:

1) If he NEVER Calls or Texts me After this Hookup, Will I be Okay?

If the answer is no, then think before you jump into bed. It's okay to turn a hot guy down. It feels like torture at the time, though. Several years ago, this super-hot actor messaged me on Grindr and asked me to hook up. He was tall, muscular, and beautiful. He was an actor, and he certainly looked the part. Without thinking, I said yes. He was a top, and generally, so am I, but I wasn't going to say no. It was painful for me, but I endured it because this guy was hot, and I wanted to date him.

But after it was over, I messaged him on Grindr and asked him if he wanted to meet for a drink sometime. You already know what's about to happen… BLOCK!

That had never happened to me before. This was about five years ago, so Grindr was still somewhat new. And I wasn't too far out of my four-year relationship. So the concept that the guy would shag me once and then cut off all communication with me was totally alien.

I was devastated. In my head, I was already married to this guy, and he just used me and blocked me like it was nothing. At the time there were loads of warning signs, but I was so distracted by his good looks that I didn't think. But again, if you hook up with someone and you feel worse afterwards, then something is wrong, and you need to think and reflect about hooking up.

2) Have you Been Honest with Yourself and the Other Guy About what the Sex Means to you?

Again, with regards to this actor, I jumped into bed with a hot guy, hoping it would lead to more, and it didn't. But on the other hand, I never asked him what he was after to ensure that we were on the same page. Now back in the pre-Grindr days, if you hooked up with someone, finding a new date might take several weeks, so it wasn't unrealistic to move things from sex to dating. But in the Grindr age, sex is just too easy.

Not too long ago, while I was in the midst of writing this book, a GORGEOUS model messaged me and was looking to hook up. Now I had chatted to this guy on and off for months. And it was obvious he was just looking for a hookup. He didn't care about me, and he didn't want to get to know me. And it was some ungodly time—like 5:00 a.m., which was a time that he may have been on drugs.

Now, I can't lie. I didn't preach at him or get on a high horse. I just politely told him, "Maybe another time," and I went back to sleep. (If you're wondering why I was awake at that time and on Grindr, I suffer from middle of the night insomnia, so I often wake up and can't get back to sleep.) Part of me thought I was nuts, turning down a gorgeous model who wanted to have sex with me. But I got that I wasn't committed to that any more. In the past, I would have done it, told him that I was fine with NSA, but I'd be secretly hoping he'd fall for me and be open to dating me. Then I'd be hurt and disappointed when he inevitably didn't feel the same way.

Shagging one more hot guy who doesn't want to date me wasn't going to alleviate whatever inner demons I was wrestling, and I was still going to be single after it was over. So I chose sleep—and my self-respect—over sex with the hot model. So be honest with yourself! If you're secretly looking for more, don't give away the milk for free.

Yes, everyone else is doing it. But you're not looking for everyone else. You're looking for the ONE. If a guy isn't keen enough to meet you in public at a reasonable hour, he's not going to be keen to be your boyfriend.

3)   Are you Guys Sexually Compatible?

I dealt with this briefly in my communication chapter, but when you're dealing with an app with all kinds of men, you need to figure out whether you're sexually compatible. Not too long ago, I matched with an insanely hot accountant named on Tinder. Guess what? He was from New Jersey, so I should have known it would end in tears. But nevertheless, I just had to meet him for a date. He was shy but cool. He kept the conversation going, and we got along.

We went home together on the first date—generally, something I don't do. But to my surprise, not only was he a top, but he was a very well-endowed one. Thinking that I'm going to marry this guy, I did my best. All things considered, I handled it pretty well. But clearly, not well enough to keep his attention. After two dates, he stopped texting. He was "pretzel" worthy, so I texted him and asked why, and he said that it was the sexual incompatibility.

First, I deserved a few more dates given how well I had done. But did he appreciate that? Nope. Again, I was left disappointed and feeling worse than before I met this guy. But had I asked him before meeting him for a date, then maybe I would have saved myself the trouble. Also, a few things he said and did gave me the impression that he might have been cheating on a potential boyfriend in the background. But again, if you just jump into bed with a pretty face, they're going to use you. So learn from my mistake.

4) When Should We Have Sex?

The previous question invites questioning at what point do you initiate sex. I, personally, almost always meet someone for a drink first, but that's in part to see whether they look like their photos. This is a personal question that only you can answer. On the one hand, you want to seem keen and strike while the "iron is hot," but on the other hand, you don't want to seem cheap. The fact is when you're in a community of all men, things are going to happen a bit faster than they would with women, as a general trend.

My rule of thumb is never have sex on a first date! I like to see if we have emotional chemistry along with physical chemistry, and that usually reveals itself on the second or third date. (I broke my own rule for the Jersey accountant, and so I got what I knew would happen. I gotta take responsibility and move on. The key is to be honest with the other guy in advance as to when you normally think things should progress to the bedroom.

I once dated a guy who told me that he had a five-date rule before he had sex. That seemed a bit excessive, but I found that I loved his personality. He had a personality that I encounter once a year or once every other year. He instantly put me at ease. He was hilarious, witty, and fun to be around. Once I met him, I was happy to wait. But had he not told me his rule, I would have concluded something was wrong after a few dates and just lost interest. Actually, on our third date, he admitted that he told people the "five date rule" just to scare away slutty guys. Any guy who knew they would have to wait several dates to get into his pants was clearly someone worth meeting. But the key was that he was open with his expectations. You have to do the same. If you don't put out for the first few dates, let the guy know that from the beginning. Yes, a great many of them will lose interest, but the ones who persevere will be keepers. But likewise, you should ask them how many dates they prefer to have before things get physical.

5)   Can you be the BEST Shag this Guy has Ever Had?

You get to decide when you're ready to have sex, but when you do, it better be AMAZING!

Remember when I said hooking up with a guy and hoping he'll want to date you afterwards usually doesn't work. There is one exception to that rule that I've found in my experience: **you have to be the best shag this guy has ever had!** Trust me; if you're giving him something that other guys won't give, he will come back. And this brings me back to the chapter title, *bring your kinky boots!* Ask this guy what he's into, and whatever he's into, you better pretend to love that. You can't hesitate; you can't qualify, and you certainly can't say "No." If he loves feet, you better pretend to love feet too. If he likes leather, you better go buy a pair of assless leather pants. Whether you guys have gone on a first date or are just hooking up, if you want to see him again, you better be the best he's ever had. Keep this in mind:

Every man has something that he loves or wants to try but he is too scared to tell you.

He may initially deny that it's there, but that's a lie so you won't think he's weird. But to the extent that you're the only person nearby willing to "give him his medicine," then he's got more reasons to stick around or come back.

In the Grindr Age, You have to be an Amazing Shag Instantly!

I realize this isn't fair, but it's true. Back in the old days, you'd have to date someone for a number of months, and eventually you'd learn each other's bodies. But in the Grindr age, people expect sexual chemistry to happen immediately because sex from other people is offered so freely and easily. You get one bite of the apple, maybe two. But that's it. If after two sexual encounters, if you haven't demonstrated that you're just as good if not better than what he can get online, then he's going to go find someone better.

"Well, my Prince Charming will wait for me." In a perfect world, he would. But that's not the world we're living in. Your Prince Charming has other people lining up to get at him. Sex is a major part of the gay lifestyle. Whether that's ideal I'll leave for a different book. But it is what's so.

6) What Are Your Red Lines?

That doesn't mean you can't have "red lines" or things you refuse to do. You have to respect yourself, your own body, and watch out for your own health. But just be clear that when you tell a man No, you are guaranteeing that he will lose interest. Maybe he was a douchebag, and it's good riddance. But if you're looking to give him a reason to call you back, then be prepared. You get to choose.

Sometimes you can say "next time," indicating that maybe you're only willing to do certain things as the relationship progresses later. But sometimes you just have to say no and be prepared to let them go.

I went on a few dates with a guy named Kinky Kevin, another actor, but he seemed sweet. He was very adamant about not having sex for the first few dates, and I respected that. But after four dates I was starting to question what was wrong. He revealed to me that he was deeply into S&M. And I don't mean light spanking or calling you "Daddy." Like heavy stuff that shocked me. And to quote Cersei Lannister, "He shocked me. Do you think I am easily shocked?"

Kevin needed to be in a leather outfit—like a complete gimp suit. He needed to have a variety of whips and chains. He needed to be physically abused while being chained up. He needed to be verbally abused just to get aroused. It was like Mr. Slave from *South Park*. It was shocking because he has a cute, innocent looking face, and he was looking for a relationship, so I wasn't sure what to do.

I never said no, but I hesitated. I asked a lot of follow up questions to see how deep his fetish went, and he picked up that I wasn't keen, so he stopped texting. In that instance, I let him go because I had a red line that I wasn't willing to cross. I want to be open-minded, but that was my limit. It was a bit sad though because Kevin is perpetually single. He's a really sweet guy, and I hope he finds his Daddy Slave Master in the not too distant future.

When it comes to sex, I wish I had an easy rule for you to adapt, but I don't. These issues are very personal and complicated. All you can do is spend some time reflecting on how you can be sexually fulfilled and identifying what you enjoy, what you're keen to try, and what you're unwilling to try. Try to keep an open mind, but you must look out for your own health and well-being. Apologies. I'm sounding like a bad Viagra commercial: "Ask your doctor if dressing up in a gimp suit is right for you."

Maybe not your doctor, but spend some time thinking or talking to a close friend. But do it **BEFORE** the super-gorgeous guy on Grindr messages you at 5:00 a.m., asking you to bring whips and chains. Because at that point, if you haven't sorted it out, you're far more likely to do something stupid that you'll later regret.

Conclusion:
This Book Works!

I recently saw the musical, *The Book of Mormon*, and although I laughed at the two hapless Mormon missionaries, I actually left with more respect for that religion than I had previously. Don't worry. You won't see me knocking at your door saying, "Hello. My name is Elder Londyn...." The point of the musical is that religion conveys useful metaphors about humanity and how we handle difficult situations. In the musical, Mormonism prospered in Africa, once everyone accepted that it's only a metaphor; they didn't take it literally. But they kept the aspects that gave them hope and inspired them to make society better in the here and now. And that's what the gay community needs right now. Moral metaphors and hope.

Trust me, I wish Lady Gaga would appear with Golden Tablets and give us a moral code to live by. But in the absence of a celebrity endorsement, all I can do is add my voice and hope my insights and perspectives prove valuable to readers who adapt them to their lives. At the risk of sounding like Tom Cruise or John Travolta, who often go on TV and proclaim "Scientology works,"[11] I want to proclaim:

Grindr Survivr Will Work For You If You Put in the Energy.

Not because I've been divinely inspired by Joseph Smith, but because change happens when you're committed to making something happen and you're actively out there doing new things,

---

[11] That's not an endorsement of Scientology, by the way. I'm just pointing out how two male celebrities, who many have speculated might not be straight, smile, charm and beg you to sign up.

rather than passively waiting and hoping for things to change—as you repeat the same behaviors endlessly.

But how am I so confident in the fact that this book works. Well, I have a secret I've held back through most of the book: I'm not single anymore. I got my man. Suck it, Grindr!

👬

I have a boyfriend and he's great! He gets me in a way that no other man I've dated ever has. He really is a spectacular guy, and I'm lucky to have him in my life. I debated about whether to mention this fact in my book. Some may read that and think, "Oh, he just said that to give me hope to increase book sales." Wrong. You've already bought the book, and I got your money. If anything, my mentioning this relationship puts more pressure on me. What if I break up with this guy in the next few months, and then I have to explain to my readers why it didn't work out? Needless to say, the re-print would be #Awkward!

To be honest, 90% of this book was written when I got into a relationship. In fact, I was so happy with my new boyfriend, I lost much of my motivation to finish it. So it languished for a few months. Then, I was unsure if I should go through and re-write sections where I refer to being single. I ultimately chose to save it for the conclusion here. But maybe that's not such a bad thing, because I want you to know, I've been where you are.

Of course, finding a man is one thing. Keeping a man is a whole other book. And I don't quite feel qualified to write that one—not yet anyway. But it's better to be in a relationship, working on developing yourself and your ability to forge intimate connections with another person rather than just sitting at home passively, annoyed that some hot guy hasn't texted you back. This book was actually never intended to be a "How to Get a Man" book," but rather a set of perspectives and techniques that empower readers to find happiness in the new world of dating apps—with or without a relationship. The point was to help you see how you were sabotaging yourself and to choose powerfully whether you wanted a solid relationship or to remain single, but in either case, you wouldn't be suffering over the gay scene anymore (and hopefully, you'll be making the Grindr scene a bit brighter).

Ideally, I hope that you will have one of two reactions to this book. First, the most common reaction is that you'll start seeing areas where you've broken the Grindr Commandments (or your own moral code as you've adapted it). And again, whether you break them is inconsequential to me, because chances are, we're not going to ever meet. But if you can see how superficial and stupid we all are throughout the dating process, you'll start to notice your bad behavior when it comes up. So just being mindful and noticing how you sabotage yourself is massive. It's like if you buy a particular brand of car, and once you start driving it, you suddenly notice all the other cars of the same make and model. There are a lot of good guys out there; you're just not looking for them with the right search criteria, and that's on you. Not them.

You're responsible for your dating life. Yes, bad things are going to happen, but the instant you let a few assholes from Jersey kill your hope for a relationship, then you're doomed. You're going to have to kiss a few frogs, even if you're seeing more clearly than ever before. But there will be far fewer major disasters because you can see the warning signs and avoid them before they escalate into full-blown gay drama.

A second reaction that is far less common would be the "A Ha!" moment. This is an epiphany! It's like riding a bicycle as a child, and you suddenly learn how to achieve balance. It's something that clicks with you. You can't perfectly describe it, but when you have it, dating suddenly becomes a lot easier, and you'll never be the same again.

You suddenly realize what a jerk you've been being and how you sabotage yourself. You will not just make an idle pledge to do better, but you will radically change how you interact with gay men. Sometimes you can get really excited if suddenly everything clicks for you. You get that gay guys are going to act like jerks, but you're excited anyway because you know in your bones that you will attract a good guy now and you will have an awesome, loving relationship! Although this type of reaction is rare, it's possible. And people with this type of epiphany make big changes, and they get big results **FAST**. But these are the people who did everything I suggested. They wrote out where they had been assholes. They apologized to people they flaked on or disappointed. They wrote out what qualities they MUST have, and they started looking for guys who had those qualities; they didn't sweat the small stuff. They dated only guys who were keen to get to know them, and they saw through the BS and lies much faster than they otherwise would have.

Neither one of these is the perfect reaction. You can be steadily noticing small changes in your behavior patterns without having a major epiphany. But in both cases, you need to be doing something NOW. If you put off any of the actions I set out, you'll just never get around to it.

The other key to making this book work for you is sharing yourself (and what you've learned from this book or in your journey through life). Now this generally is **NOT** an appropriate type of conversation to have on the apps or even on a first date. You'd have this with a close friend or a relative you trust, one who will give you honest feedback while not judging you for sharing your own negative traits. Talking and sharing about where you are in your own journey does two things: First, if your friend is smart, they can help you identify your own blind spots. Second, when you articulate your recent reflections and new actions out loud, you'll notice that you may have accomplished way more than what you thought you could. It may not seem big to you in the moment when you did it, but as you explain the situation to a friend, you'll think "Oh wow. That's pretty cool that I did that." Also, when you have to share your defeats or moral quandaries, you'll also see more quickly all the areas where you've been acting like a jerk or sabotaging yourself. There's something about saying it out loud in front of another person that allows you to see whether you're being a douche or whether you're merely just chasing one.

As gays, we're really good at telling each other how some asshole did us wrong, but we're not so good at sharing where we've been jerks and how we made amends.

So here are your final rules from me:

Action Point:
For every time you complain about a gay guy "out there," reveal two things about yourself!

Identify two areas where you broke the Grindr Commandments or didn't live up to your own moral code. Or share how you were responsible for chasing after someone that you knew was trouble. You're still responsible for that part. Look for instances where you did something thoughtless (if not overtly mean), passed on a nice guy who wasn't hot enough, or gave yourself a stupid excuse for flaking or not texting back. There's no power in being a victim. Just learn from sharing your mistakes out loud, and you'll be far less likely to repeat them.

Action Point:
Share your Victories!

As you get better at changing yourself, you'll make better choices, and that's worth celebrating. Every good choice you make is eliminating one probable instance of sitting at home crying, and it may bring you one step closer to finding the man who's right for you. You might spot a psycho much quicker, or you will feel good about apologizing to someone. Share that with a close friend. That's a big deal. People don't have epiphanies every day (or even small ones). You'll only pull yourself out of cynicism by taking action to change your life and then sharing your results with friends who are supportive. The key is to keep sharing where you're at, so you keep growing and developing.

What I don't want is for people to read this book, thinking "I agree with 90% of what he said" and then put the book down, take no action, and go back to being a Sleeping Beauty or a Mindless Shag Zombie. If you're going to do that, then at least be real with yourself. Tell yourself, "If I continue to do the same thing over and over again, I'm going to get the same result, but that's OKAY!" You survived Grindr this long, and you'll continue to survive. Embrace who you are and where you're at in the dating process. If you want some time to be young and free, then go for it. That by itself can be an epiphany because it can take a weight off of your shoulders. You'll be single, because you want to be single, rather than being a victim of vapid gays who won't call you back.

But the point of the book isn't just to give you the result that you want; it's to shift your mentality around dating altogether, and that's why I think I've got a great relationship. Not because I got lucky, but because I was able to see things more clearly than I did at the beginning of writing this book.

This book first started as a blog where I would just vent about shitty things that happened to me online and yell into the ether that gay guys shouldn't be such dickheads. And of course, by venting, I felt better. But as I continued to write and reflect on what I wanted to say, I had to be fair to my readers, and I saw I had a duty to examine my own behavior in the process. I saw that I was no saint. Although I rarely did anything obnoxious, I was often thoughtless. And I was much more superficial than I previously realized.

So when I decided to start writing this book, I had to dig deeper. It took a significant amount of time to analyze my behavior, assess the behavior of others, reflect on what didn't work, find lessons I could learn from, search for areas where I was acting like a jerk and didn't know it, and then carefully articulate all of my insights to complete strangers. Whew! That's exhausting. But in writing this book, I saw these principles much more clearly. It was easier to size people up, embrace the ones who were keen to get to know me, and move on from the ones that weren't (even if they were super-hot). That's what put me in the right mentality to find an awesome relationship, and now, you can do that too!

But the key is take action. Don't just think and reflect: share yourself, do new and different things. You've done it the old way, so now it's time for something new. I hope my book has given you some insights into yourself, and, hopefully, it will inspire you to elevate the conversation of the entire gay community. One book isn't enough to solve all of your dating problems, but it's a good place to start if you're willing to do something about it.

Thank You!

Thank you so much for reading all of this. You don't know me, and I don't know you. Yet you took a chance on a complete stranger. You took my advice with an open mind, even though you didn't know a thing about me. You considered some radical proposals I made, and you also looked at yourself in a new light, and a lot of it was not pretty. Hopefully, you are now going to take action and transform your dating life. These are not conversations people ordinarily have in everyday life. And they are definitely not typical conversations we have on Grindr. But wouldn't it be cool if we could? Wouldn't it be cool if we could use apps to connect emotionally as well as physically? Grindr is just a technological app; it's only as good or as bad as the people who use it. And you've just demonstrated that you're up for way more than what you thought possible at the beginning of the book. You're going to do great things. Thanks for letting me play a small role in your own personal journey.

One Last Favor...

If you found the book helpful, I'd greatly appreciate your positive review on Amazon (or on iTunes). Writing a review on Amazon is a great way to share new insights into yourself and positive results you've created. But even if you think I missed something or that I was totally wrong, I'd love to hear about that too—so long as you at least carefully considered what I proposed and did some of the exercises. I read all of the reviews, and ultimately it's about our thinking and growing as human beings. Even online conversations can make a difference.

I wrote this with no backing or support from any publishing company. I took a lot of my free time to write it, and I had to pay myself for someone to help me with the cover and other illustrations, the editing, the conversion into eBook formatting, etc. But in writing this book, I discovered a new passion for writing and a genuine commitment to help gay men get what they want from their dating lives. So if you found value, a positive review will help others get the same benefit.

And don't forget social media:

#GrindrCode, #GrindrCommandments, and #GayCommandments

If enough people start using these hashtags, things will change online. Yes, it seems corny now, but if enough people start doing it, new standards will become normal, and isn't that what we want? Wouldn't it be a great way to signal to potential dates that you're genuine and you reflect on your behavior and live by a higher code than what's available today on Grindr? And wouldn't it be refreshing if you could see this in other potential dates when you messaged them online? Wouldn't it be cool to know that the guy you're messaging has at least spent several hours reflecting on his own behavior, improved his attitude towards dating and has committed himself not to act like a douche or another Shagging Zombie? Again, I'm open to other ideas about how gay guys can quickly signal to each other that they're looking for more, and they're ready for something better than what's currently offered online, but until then, this is a great way to start, so let's make it happen!

Printed in Great Britain
by Amazon